Dawn of an Empire

Dawn of an Empire

St. Augustine and the Spanish Founding of America

By Irene Loftin
Unbound Press

Dawn of an Empire: St. Augustine and the Spanish Founding of America

Series: America Uncovered, By Irene Loftin

compliance with local laws and professional standards in their jurisdiction. This edition reflects information available as of [February 2026].

References to real organizations, products, devices, or services are for identification only and do not imply endorsement or affiliation. When research findings or statistics are cited, sources are provided in notes or references. The absence of a citation does not imply universal consensus.

ISBN Paperback 978-1-971207-21-6
ISBN Hardcover 978-1-971207-22-3

America Uncovered:

This series uncovers the hidden foundations of American cities: who built them, who controlled them, who was erased from their origin stories, and how competing empires, cultures, and peoples shaped the ground we stand on today.

Each volume focuses on a single place at a decisive moment—Spanish, French, Indigenous, African, British, or American—revealing how conquest, diplomacy, slavery, resistance, and ambition forged the city's identity long before it became part of the United States.

These are not romantic origin tales, but lost structural beginnings. Each book stands alone, but together they reconstruct a national pattern: America as an imperial project layered over Indigenous land, contested by global powers, and built by people whose names rarely made it into textbooks.

Table of Contents

Dedication

For the forgotten founders of St. Augustine, whose stories shaped America long before America knew its own name.

And for the generations who inherit this ground, may you look deeper, ask harder questions, and never mistake myth for history.

Look to the past and remember no empire rises that sooner or later won't fall.

—Al Stewart

Introduction

The Beginning We Were Taught

Ask most Americans where their country began, and the answer comes easily: Plymouth Rock. Jamestown. A narrow strip of the Atlantic coast where English settlers struggled, endured, and, so the story goes, gave birth to a nation. This version of the past is familiar, comforting, and incomplete.

The truth is that America did not begin there. America's first real "founding fathers" did not answer to names like Washington or Adams. Their names were Pedro Menéndez de Avilés, who sailed into a mosquito-thick harbor in 1565 and claimed it for Spain; Francisco López de Mendoza Grajales, who celebrated the first recorded Catholic Mass in what is now the continental United States; and Martín de Argüelles Jr., born in 1566, the first documented child of European descent born on what would become American soil.

From the beginning, it was not an English story. It was Spanish soldiers and sailors. It was Africans—both enslaved and free—who sustained the colony through their labor and skill, and whose descendants would shape its future. It was Italians and Greeks recruited to farm the frontier in the eighteenth century, Germans seeking opportunity, and Irish priests serving a Catholic outpost on the edge of Protestant North America. It was the Timucua,

Guale, and Apalachee peoples, whose towns predated any European claim and whose alliances, resistance, and endurance defined the region's fate. This is not a footnote.

It is a different origin story.

More than forty years before Jamestown and more than half a century before Plymouth, a permanent European settlement already existed on the North American mainland. It was established not by English Protestants seeking liberty but by Spanish Catholics securing empire. It was multiracial, militarized, hierarchical, and durable. And it has been largely written out of the national story.

That place was St. Augustine.

When we say America was "multicultural," we think of the decades-long melting-pot immigration. But St. Augustine was multilingual and multiethnic from the outset. Spanish commanders governed Indigenous allies, African militia members defended the town's walls, and intermarriage blurred categories that later centuries would try to harden. In 1738, just north of the city, Spain sanctioned Fort Mose, the first legally recognized free Black settlement in what would become the United States—a refuge for people escaping British slavery.

That changes things.

It unsettles the tidy narrative that America began as an English Protestant experiment and later became diverse. It complicates the idea that immigration is a modern disruption of an original cultural purity. There was no purity. There was collision, negotiation, coercion, and adaptation—right from the start.

If the first permanent European city in the continental United States was already African, Indigenous, Mediterranean, and Atlantic in character, then race in America was not born in a vacuum of sameness. It was forged in proximity. Immigration was not an afterthought. It was foundational. St. Augustine was America's first true melting pot—before the phrase existed and before the myth of homogeneity took hold.

And yet, almost no one remembers.

Founded in 1565, St. Augustine is the oldest continuously occupied European-founded city in the United States. This is not a disputed claim. It is a documented fact. Yet for most Americans, St. Augustine is remembered—if at all—as a tourist destination, a regional curiosity, or a historical footnote. It is rarely treated as foundational.

We celebrate Plymouth Rock, reenact Jamestown, and teach the thirteen colonies as the beginning. Meanwhile, the city that predates them all endures quietly on Florida's coast, its streets older than the nation, its story folded into shadow. Recovering this beginning is not to diminish what came later. It is to widen the lens. America did not begin as a single thread gradually weaving in others. It began as a knot—tight, contested, entangled from the first moment.

This book begins with a simple yet provocative question: How did the first enduring colony in American history, St. Augustine, disappear from the nation's collective memory?

The answer is not ignorance, but selection.

The United States inherited its origin story from those who won power—political, cultural, and intellectual—after independence. That story privileged the English language, Protestant belief, and narratives of self-rule. Spanish Florida fit none of those categories. It represented empire before nationhood, Catholic authority before dissent, and racial complexity before the rigid binaries that later defined American law and identity.

St. Augustine complicates the story Americans know. It forces a reckoning with the fact that America began not as an experiment in liberty but as a contested imperial frontier. Africans—enslaved and free—were present from the beginning. Indigenous peoples were not merely obstacles to settlement but participants in alliances, resistance, and survival. That continuity, not rebellion, was the first defining feature of life on this land under European rule.

Acknowledging St. Augustine as foundational is not to celebrate the Spanish empire or to replace one myth with another. It is to recognize that the United States did not emerge from a single moral arc or cultural tradition. Instead, it emerged from a collision among empires, peoples, religions, and systems of power.

History is not just what happened. It is what is remembered, taught, and elevated. St. Augustine was not forgotten by accident. It was sidelined because it unsettled the story Americans wanted to tell about themselves. This book restores that beginning—not to diminish Jamestown or Plymouth, but to place them where they belong: after. If we are serious about understanding America—its contradictions, its hierarchies, its unfinished struggles—we must start where the story actually begins, not with pilgrims or pioneers, but with a stone fortress on the Florida coast, built to last, and a colony that refused to disappear.

The pages that follow return American history to its true starting point and ask what changes when we do.

Part I — Before the English

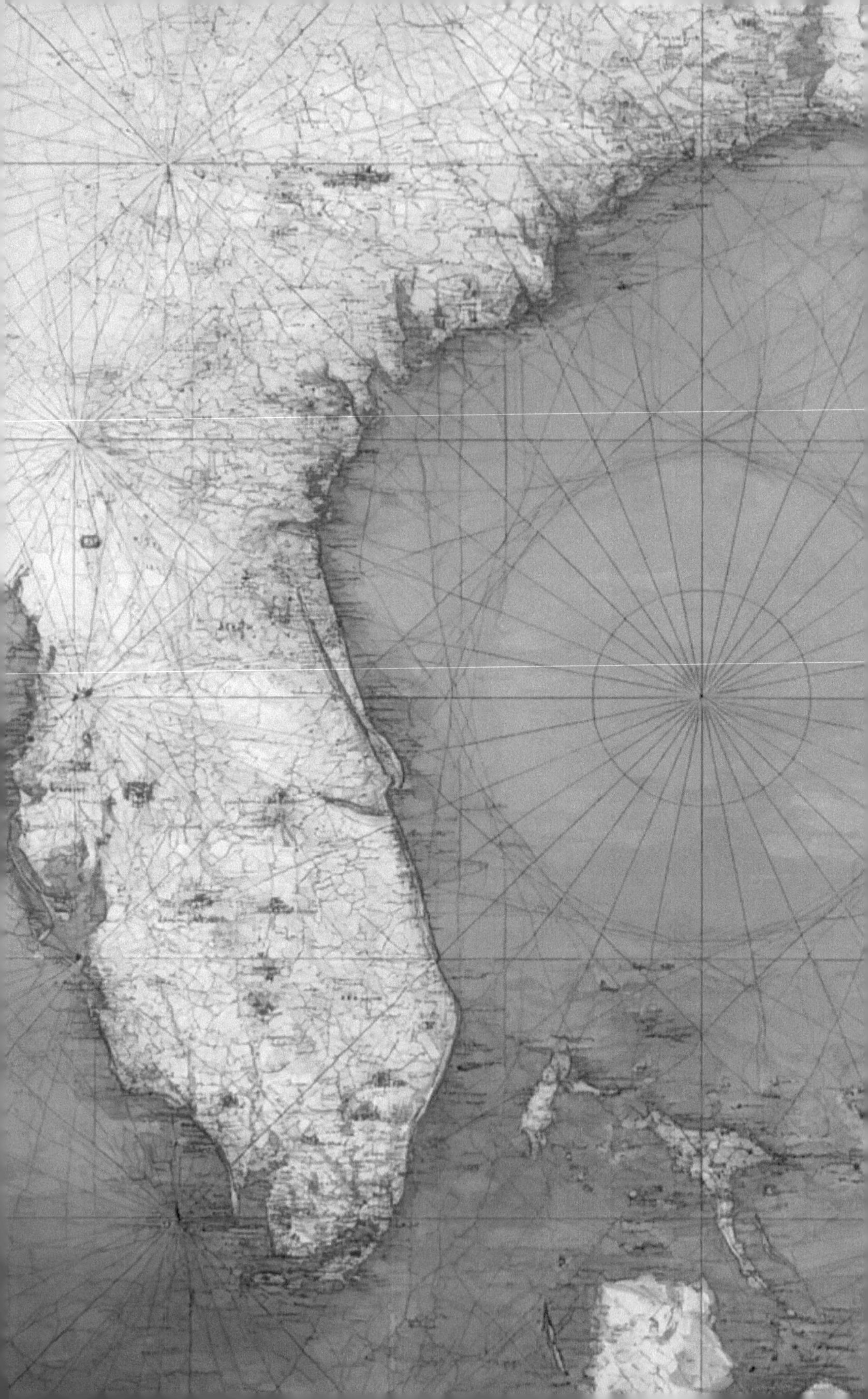

1

America Begins in Florida

Great conquests trouble, where contempt may please -- the one yields glory, and the other ease.

—William Alexander, 1st Earl of Stirling

The Siege No One Remembers

THE CANNONS BEGAN AT dawn.

The air smelled of wet powder and smoke rising through the palmettos as the first blast broke the silence. The bone-shaking thud of the guns rolling over the earth shattered the humid stillness, and the world trembled—each explosion sending sand skyward, each recoil thumping the ground like distant thunder.

The British flag still flew over Fort George, snapping in the Gulf wind, but the ground beneath it belonged to someone else. Spanish artillery, hauled through swamps and pine barrens, had advanced for weeks. Trenches zigzagged toward the British lines, sand slick with spring rain and powder smoke. This was Pensacola—the capital of British West Florida and what Britain called its fourteenth royal colony in North America. It was a colony most Americans have never heard of, and it was about to fall.

In the spring of 1781, just months before Yorktown, while General Washington watched and waited in the north and British redcoats marched through the Carolinas, a parallel war raged under the punishing Gulf Coast sun. As American fortunes shifted around Virginia, the siege of Pensacola unfolded far to the south, bearing little resemblance to the Revolution of familiar history books. Here, no famous portraits awaited painting, and no frontiersmen or patriots crouched behind stone walls. There was only mud, mosquitoes, and the steady barrage of Spanish artillery pounding the British fleet.

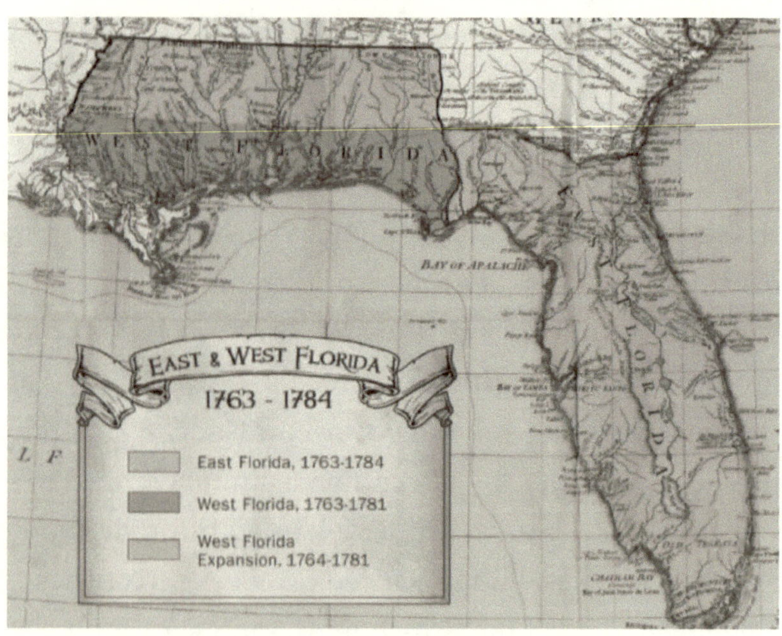

Map of East and West Florida c 1763

Florida entered the war not as a rebellious partner to the Patriot cause but as a recent imperial prize. In 1763, following the Seven Years' War, Spain handed Florida to

Britain in exchange for Havana. The transfer reshaped the Gulf Coast overnight. What had been a sprawling but loosely held Spanish province became two new British colonies: East Florida and West Florida.

West Florida stretched from the Mississippi to the Apalachicola River, including parts of present-day Louisiana, Mississippi, Alabama, and the Florida Panhandle. Pensacola—a modest but strategic port— became its capital. East Florida ran from the Apalachicola River across the peninsula to the Atlantic Ocean. Its capital was St. Augustine—by then a settlement of several hundred buildings and thousands of permanent residents who had weathered two centuries of storms, sieges, and shifting flags.

When we picture the American Revolution, we imagine thirteen colonies strung along the Atlantic seaboard. Yet in 1776, there were not 13 British colonies in North America but 15. Florida, divided into East and West, did not join the rebellion. The 14th and 15th colonies remained loyal to the Crown, making Pensacola more than a distant outpost; it became a pivot point in a war that would span oceans and continents.

Spain held no formal alliance with the Patriots but rather had entered the conflict as an enemy of Britain after decades of conflict between the two nations. Spanish forces struck British positions along the Mississippi, seized Baton Rouge and Mobile, and now laid siege to Pensacola, the last British stronghold on the Gulf.

Yet across these contested coasts and river valleys, Native nations such as the Timucua, Calusa, and Choctaw weighed their own interests and shifted alliances, sometimes negotiating with Spanish or British commanders and at other times resisting encroachment from both. For these Indigenous nations, the siege was not simply a struggle between rival European empires but another moment in an ongoing fight to defend land and autonomy in a volatile borderland.

We are told the American Revolution was fought in Boston, Saratoga, and Yorktown. But we do not remember that Spain—operating from Louisiana, Cuba, and Florida— helped break Britain's southern flank. Florida was not an empty backwater during the Revolution but strategic, contested ground. In fact, the oldest permanent European city in what is now the United States was not British at all. It was Spanish.

The narrative of English ships, English charters, and English settlers carving a future from the wilderness is tidy, linear, and Protestant. But that is not where this continent's European chapter began. More than four decades before Jamestown, Spain had already planted its standard on the Florida coast and built a settlement that would endure. The city was San Agustín.

From that beginning, Florida became a bargaining chip in European diplomacy and a frontier laboratory where Spain tested the mechanics of empire in North America. On the maps drafted in Madrid, Florida appeared as a tidy expanse of color—an imperial possession rendered in confident ink. But the cartographers had never felt the ground shift beneath their feet. This was a borderland that refused to hold still. The flags above St. Augustine and Pensacola changed four times in sixty years.

Yet beneath the pageantry of empire, something more enduring persisted. The mechanics of survival, the networks of trade, the accommodations among peoples, and the knowledge of how to wrest a living from this unforgiving coast ground on regardless of which monarch's portrait hung in the governor's hall.

And yet it sits in the margins of the American story. Why?

Partly because it was Catholic instead of Protestant. Partly because it was Spanish rather than English, and partly because, when Britain briefly took Florida in 1763, the Spanish chapter was inconvenient to the narrative of Patriotic destiny. But mostly because history is often written by those who inherit the power and the language of the winners.

The standard story ignores two centuries of Spanish maps, missions, and fortresses pressed into the sand. Public memory is shaped not just by what happened, but by which stories are chosen to fill the pages and classrooms. Yet the old Spanish city, ever worn and watchful, endured.

Spanish America

To understand the significance of Pensacola and St. Augustine, we need to step back in time—beyond the Revolution and British rule. Rewind two centuries to when Spain's empire stretched across the Atlantic, and Florida was not an afterthought but a frontier of faith, gold, and empire. Before the Pilgrims and the Mayflower. Before the word "American" meant what it would one day come to mean. The dawn of an empire did not break in Massachusetts or Virginia: it began as Spain's dream of settling a new territory more than 4,000 miles across the ocean.

1513 — Ponce de León and The First Claim

Before there was a fort on a European map, there was a shoreline. In the spring of 1513, a fleet of three small ships approached land along Florida's Atlantic coast.[1] They were the Santiago, the San Cristóbal, and the Santa María de la Consolación.

When Juan Ponce de León sighted the land, he named it La Florida—likely for the Easter season, Pascua Florida, and for the lushness that met his eyes from the deck. He claimed it for the Spanish Crown. That act, the simple ritual of raising a banner and reading a declaration, transformed inhabited land into imperial property in the eyes of European law. And it would redraw centuries of human history on the peninsula.

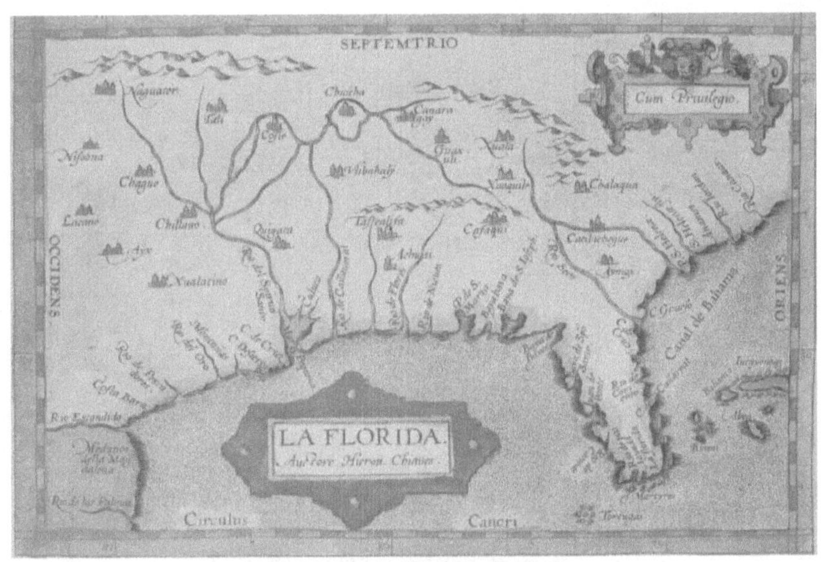

Map of La Florida, 1513

The land Ponce de León claimed was vast and undefined. "La Florida" in 1513 did not resemble the modern state. It referred broadly to the southeastern portion of North America—at times stretching well beyond today's peninsula. Maps would shrink and stretch the borders for decades as knowledge caught up with ambition. The 1513 voyage also did not establish a permanent settlement. It was reconnaissance—mapping coastlines, noting currents, identifying anchorages, and making contact, sometimes violently, with local populations.

The claim was intentionally elastic; by keeping boundaries vague, Spain could later argue that the land had always been theirs. In 1513, Spain was not exploring solely for wonder or curiosity. It was consolidating power.

The conquest of the Caribbean was already underway, and the Spanish Crown had tasted the possibilities of empire. Gold was being exported from Puerto Rico (Hispaniola), and it wanted more: more land, more labor, more souls to convert, and more strategic advantage over rival European powers.

Florida offered Spain three temptations—each powerful enough on its own, irresistible together.

First, geography. The peninsula jutted into the Atlantic like a bent elbow, curving protectively around the Bahama Channel, a tight, fast-moving corridor that funneled ships leaving the Caribbean north before they caught the Gulf Stream home to Europe. In 1513, the treasure fleets had not yet reached their later scale, but the pattern was already forming: silver and gold would move through these waters. So would sugar, hides, dyes, and human cargo.

Control Florida, and you did not merely possess land. You watched the sea and guarded the artery through which imperial wealth would eventually pulse. If Florida were unattended, you left the empire's throat exposed.

Second, resources—real or imagined. Spain's Atlantic expansion was fueled as much by rumor as by proven riches. Word traveled ahead of proof. Stories of wealthy northern chiefdoms circulated among sailors and settlers in the Caribbean. Mexico and Peru had already shown what was possible when rumor met conquest. Florida, poorly mapped yet vast in European imagination, might be the threshold to another inland empire. Or, at the very least, it might yield labor, timber, pitch, and tar—whatever could be extracted and shipped.

The point was not certainty, but possibility. And possibility was enough to justify another voyage.

Illustration, Map of Atlantic Coast

Third, prestige and preemption. In the early sixteenth century, empire was a race carried out across the water. France probed the Atlantic as England watched. An unclaimed coastline was an invitation. A harbor left undefended was a future rival's foothold. Claim early, and you establish precedent. With precedent, you possess an argument when diplomats draw lines on maps decades later. In this Atlantic world, absence was dangerous. To be missing from a coastline was to concede it.

Florida, then, was not a wilderness curiosity but a strategic maritime shield. It was a wager on wealth and a line in the sand drawn before anyone else could draw theirs first.

Ponce de León's time in Florida was brief. He landed somewhere along the eastern shore, then charted the Atlantic coast down to the Florida Keys and north along the Gulf coast. In that first moment, Florida was not yet a place you could hold. It was a coastline you could name, a set of bearings you could record, and proof you could carry back across the sea.

The true prize of the voyage was not the sand under his boots but the argument he could later make at court. A man could "find" land and still lose it to a better-connected rival unless the Crown sealed his rights in ink. If Florida was going to become his project, he needed to move quickly.

So he did the most practical thing imaginable: he left Florida behind and went to Spain. In Seville, those discoveries became documents. At the Casa de Contratación, the empire's bureaucrats took his reports, revised their master charts, and incorporated Florida into the official geography of Spanish power. The Atlantic coast became a line on the Padrón Real. The idea of Florida hardened first in maps and paperwork, long before it hardened into a fort.

Ponce de León won what explorers always seek: authorization. But empire is never only about ambition; it is about timing. When his patron, King Ferdinand, died in 1516, court politics shifted beneath his feet. Claims had to be defended again, and grants re-argued. While he waited, other Spaniards treated "Florida" the way frontier men often do: as a place to raid, a place to take.

1521 — The First Settlement

By the time he set sail in 1521, Juan Ponce de León was not chasing a mythical fountain. He carried a royal license to establish a colony. The paperwork was explicit: claim the land, build a settlement, and make Spain's presence permanent. He needed to turn the previous claim into a foothold. To the Crown, it was a possession waiting to be secured.

He brought roughly 200 colonists, primarily adult men, along with priests, craftsmen, farmers, horses, and livestock. This was not a scouting mission. It was an attempt to root Spain in Florida soil, to turn rumor into acreage and coastline into empire.

What they sought was tangible: land to cultivate, authority to wield, and—if fortune favored them—gold.

Florida was envisioned as the next extension of Spain's expanding Atlantic world, a place that might yield wealth or at least secure Spain's strategic reach.

They stepped onto Florida's southwest coast, likely somewhere near present-day Charlotte Harbor, with animals, tools, and seeds. The choreography of colonization was familiar by then: land, fortify, plant, convert. The land would yield crops, and the people would yield labor. Spain would gain a foothold on the peninsula that guarded the empire's sea lanes.

Timucua People

But Florida was not an empty stage. For millennia, Florida's coast had been surf and low dunes, and villages that watched from a distance.

This land was already owned by people who did not recognize the authority of a distant king. Florida was home to complex Indigenous societies—Timucua in the north and east, Calusa in the southwest, Apalachee in the panhandle, and others whose political networks predated Spanish contact by centuries. These were not scattered bands but organized communities with agriculture, trade routes, and spiritual systems deeply rooted in place.

Before Flags

Before Spain named Florida, it already had another name. Not on parchment or in royal decrees, but in rivers, fishing grounds, and pathways cut through pine flatwoods. Before the missions, forts, and sieges, Florida was already ordered, governed, and claimed. Their authority came not from a distant monarch but from generations of lived presence in the peninsula's rivers, forests, and Gulf waters. To tell Florida's story honestly, we begin here—not with a flag, but with the people already there.

Geography as Government

Florida's geography did not merely shape Indigenous life; it structured it. The peninsula is long and narrow, threaded with rivers, wetlands, pine barrens, and coastal shallows. Movement followed water, and power followed food sources. No single polity controlled the entire region because the land itself resisted centralization.

In the north, agriculture fostered denser settlement and mound-building hierarchies. In the southwest, fisheries supported centralized maritime authority. In the interior, dispersed communities relied on seasonal mobility and kin networks. Political systems were tuned to ecology — resilient, sometimes rivalrous, and always pragmatic. Alliances shifted. Trade routes linked the Gulf to the Atlantic. Copper, shell, and ritual objects moved through networks older than European navigation in these waters. When Spain arrived, it did not encounter an empty coastline or wilderness. It encountered competitors.

The Timucua — The North and the Interior

The Timucua lived across northern Florida and into what is now southern Georgia. They were not a single centralized nation but a constellation of chiefdoms bound by language and cultural ties. Their world followed the rivers.

The St. Johns, the Suwannee, the inland lakes, and the marshes were not obstacles; they were highways. Villages were often positioned near waterways, and authority rested with local chiefs who governed through kinship networks and reciprocal obligations. Power was personal, negotiated, and embedded in ritual and redistribution.

A chief held influence because he could protect, feed, and mediate. Ceremonial centers reinforced hierarchy, but survival depended on cooperation. Agriculture, especially maize, was established in many areas, and hunting, fishing, and gathering supplemented it. The landscape was not wild in the European sense; it was managed, strategically burned, and cultivated in patterns refined over generations.

When Europeans later described Florida as thinly settled, they misunderstood what they saw. The Timucuan political organization was regional rather than imperial. It did not announce itself with walls of stone, but it was durable, adaptable, and deeply rooted.

Eastern Timucua

The Eastern Timucua occupied the Atlantic-facing world—stretching along the northeastern Florida coast and into the Sea Islands of what is now southeastern Georgia. They lived along the St. Johns River and its tributaries, as well as among the tidal rivers, swamps, and inland forests that extended toward the Okefenokee. Their villages clustered near waterways using rivers as boundaries.

Their lifeways reflected that ecology. They fished in tidal estuaries, harvested shellfish, hunted along wetland margins, and cultivated maize in nearby clearings. Pottery styles, mound construction, and settlement patterns reflect a long continuity of adaptation to marine and freshwater environments.

Along the Atlantic edge of Timucua country, the most powerful and best-documented communities were the Mocama. They lived in the tidal world of barrier islands, river mouths, and estuaries stretching from present-day St. Simons Island south to the mouth of the St. Johns River. The Spanish later called this stretch the Mocama Province, one of the principal divisions of their mission system. The name itself came from the people: Mocama—"Ocean."

Their dialect of the Timucua language is the best preserved, largely because missionaries recorded it with unusual care.

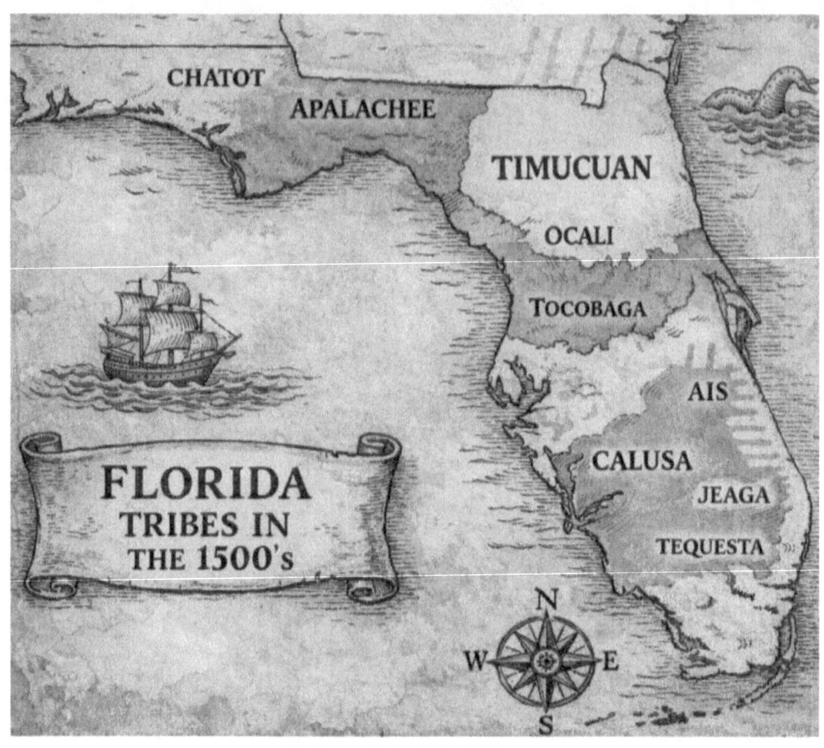

Map of Florida Tribes

At the time of European contact, two major chiefdoms anchored Mocama power: the Saturiwa and the Tacatacuru.

The Saturiwa were centered on the mouth of the St. Johns River, in what is now Jacksonville. Their principal village stood on the river's south bank. Farther north, on Cumberland Island in present-day Georgia, the Tacatacuru controlled coastal settlements and waterways. They were eventually incorporated into the Spanish orbit. In 1587, Mission San Pedro de Mocama was founded, directly linking their island world to St. Augustine's expanding religious and political framework.

Beyond these two major chiefdoms lay a mosaic of other Eastern Timucua communities. North of the Satilla River on the Georgia mainland lived the Icafui and Cascangue, speakers of the Itafi dialect. Opposite Cumberland Island lived the Yufera, whose dialect bore their name. Inland were the Ibi, organized into five towns about fifty miles from the coast.

Farther west, possibly along the eastern edge of the Okefenokee Swamp, the Oconi lived. Over time, many of these communities were also drawn into mission life— some received their own churches, while others were placed under the supervision of coastal missions such as San Pedro.

South along the St. Johns River from the Saturiwa were the Utina, later known in Spanish sources as the Agua Dulce or Agua Fresca—the "Freshwater" people. They occupied the river corridor from the Palatka region south toward Lake George and participated in the broader St. Johns cultural tradition. In the 1560s, the Utina chiefdom was formidable—more than forty villages lay under its influence. The stretch of river between them and the Saturiwa appears to have been sparsely settled, perhaps serving as a buffer zone between rival powers frequently at war.

Western Timucua

If the Eastern Timucua lived by tide and estuary, the Western Timucua lived by river valley and upland forest.

Three major western groupings—the Potano, the Northern Utina, and the Yustaga—would, over the late sixteenth and seventeenth centuries, be drawn into the expanding orbit of Spanish missions. Yet incorporation did not mean uniformity. Like its eastern counterparts, each brought its own political structure, rivalries, and survival strategy into that colonial encounter.

Illustration, Timucua People

The Potano occupied north-central Florida, centered in what is now Alachua County, extending west toward the Suwannee River. Archaeologists associate them with the Alachua cultural tradition. They were among the earliest Timucua to confront Europeans directly.[2]

Warfare defined much of their sixteenth-century history. They were frequently at odds with the Utina, who successfully courted both French and Spanish alliances in campaigns against them. North of the Potano, stretching between the Suwannee and St. Johns Rivers, lived the people later labeled by historians as the Northern Utina. To their contemporaries, they were simply known as "Timucua." They spoke what scholars often call the Timucua proper dialect and were linked to the Suwannee Valley cultural sphere. Unlike the more centralized Mocama chiefdoms on the coast, the Northern Utina appear to have been organized into several smaller local chiefdoms, with one paramount leader.

Across the Suwannee River—the natural boundary separating them from the Northern Utina—lived the westernmost Timucuan communities: the Yustaga and the Asile. The Yustaga occupied territory between the Suwannee and the Aucilla River, which marked the frontier with the powerful Apalachee. They shared many cultural traits with the Suwannee Valley world but may have spoken a distinct dialect. Unlike many of their Timucua neighbors, the Yustaga resisted Spanish missionary efforts well into the seventeenth century. Their more limited early contact with Europeans likely shielded them, at least temporarily, from the full force of epidemic disease, allowing them to retain higher population levels longer than many other Timucua groups.

Other Western Timucua groups flicker in the earliest records and then disappear. The Ocale, whose name survives in modern Ocala, lived in the interior of present-day Marion County. They were encountered—and likely shattered—during Hernando de Soto's 1539 expedition.[3] Later French and Spanish sources mention a town named Eloquale in the Acuera chiefdom, suggesting that surviving Ocale communities may have migrated eastward and merged with neighbors.

The Timucua were not only providers; they were also a literate people in the colonial record. Missionaries, especially Francisco Pareja in the early 1600s, produced substantial printed works in Timucua—catechisms and a grammar—making it one of the best-documented and earliest extensively written-and-printed Indigenous languages of the early Southeast.[4]

What emerges from this western landscape is not a uniform people but a layered interior world of river valleys, upland forests, and borderlands, where chiefdoms rose and fell, migrated, merged, and resisted.

The Apalachee — The Agricultural Power of the Gulf Coast

To the west, in the pine uplands and red clay soils of the panhandle, the Apalachee held one of the most formidable agricultural centers in the Southeast.

Their lands were fertile, and maize production supported dense populations compared with much of the peninsula.

Politically, they were part of the broader Mississippian cultural sphere—hierarchical, ceremonial, and capable of organizing large communities around mound centers.

Apalachee Tribe village

The Apalachee were not peripheral players. When Spanish expeditions marched inland in the 1500s, they encountered warrior societies capable of sustaining winter encampments and negotiating—or resisting—from a position of strength. This was Gulf Florida's breadbasket. Control here meant food. And food meant leverage.

The Tocobaga and the Central Gulf

The Tocobaga lived around Tampa Bay, part of a broader network of Gulf Coast communities linked by trade and shared ecological knowledge. Their settlements often clustered around mounds overlooking bays and estuaries. The Gulf was both pantry and pathway. Like the Calusa, they were masters of marine environments, but politically they were less centralized—more confederated, with shifting alliances as conditions required.

The Calusa of the Southwest

While north Florida was riverine and agricultural, southwest Florida belonged to water. The Calusa built their power not on maize fields but on fisheries. They controlled the estuaries, mangrove labyrinths, and barrier islands along the Gulf. Massive engineered shell mounds rose as both refuse and architecture. Canoes were not tools; they were instruments of dominance.

La Florida Map of Native Nations c 1550

The Calusa organized into a centralized political structure more cohesive than those of many of their northern neighbors. A paramount chief governed subordinate communities. Tribute flowed inward, and authority radiated outward across waterways rather than farmland. To approach the southwest coast without permission was to enter a defended maritime kingdom.

The Balance Before Disruption

The native power structures of Florida had weathered storms, droughts, migrations, and conflict. What they had not encountered before the sixteenth century was the particular combination Spain brought: steel, horses, epidemic disease, and a legal doctrine that declared land transferable by proclamation.

That collision would transform everything.

❖

When Juan Ponce de León's ships arrived on Florida's coast in 1521, carrying settlers and supplies, they were not alone. They met the Calusa, who had no reason to welcome foreigners. Spain came ashore with the posture of settlement, transporting people, animals, and tools. That posture itself was a threat. Whatever his plan for planting a Spanish foothold, it depended on time: time to unload, build, fortify, and find food. The Calusa understood what the Spaniards were attempting before the Spaniards could complete it.

Juan Ponce de León

Resistance came fast. Within days, the expedition was under attack. Arrows flew; the landing turned into a fight for survival. Ponce de León was struck and wounded in the thigh—and with him went the venture's momentum. A colony cannot be born while its leader bleeds and its perimeter is collapsing. The colony, barely born, collapsed under pressure. The settlers pulled back to their ships and retreated to Cuba.

Ponce de León died soon after, likely from infection, and the settlement attempt died with him. But failure did not erase the claim. Madrid recalculated and reorganized, and five years later, Spain tried again—this time on a larger scale.

1526 — Lucas Vázquez de Ayllón and The Second Attempt

Lucas Vázquez de Ayllón was not a conquistador in armor but a royal lawyer—precisely the kind of man the Spanish Crown needed. Under King Ferdinand, he had become an influential political figure on the island of San Domingo— part magistrate, part entrepreneur, and fully embedded in the machinery of empire.

In 1521, a slaving ship commissioned by Ayllón, intended for the Bahamas, instead sailed northwest. On June 24, 1521, he reached Winyah Bay along the coast of present-day South Carolina. There, after brief exploration, he and his crew kidnapped approximately sixty Native people and carried them back to Hispaniola. Along with the captives, they brought reports of fertile land that, they claimed, would not require large-scale military conquest and could become a prosperous colony.

Ayllón acted quickly. He petitioned the Crown for the right to explore and settle the region on Spain's behalf. He personally advanced his case in Madrid and brought with him one of the captives, baptized Francisco de Chicora, whose descriptions of the land helped shape the proposal. On June 12, 1523, Ayllón secured a royal contract authorizing him to establish a settlement along North America's eastern seaboard and to trade with its inhabitants.

Ayllón staked everything on the venture. He poured much of his personal fortune into it and went into debt to outfit a true settlement fleet of six ships carrying roughly 600 to 700 people. This was no raiding party. This time, among the passengers were women and children, along with Black enslaved people, priests, craftsmen, and laborers. They loaded livestock—cattle, sheep, and pigs— and about one hundred horses, the mobile muscle of Spanish expansion.

In mid-July 1526, the fleet sailed and on August 9 entered Winyah Bay. Almost immediately, disaster struck: the largest ship ran aground on a sandbar and sank. No lives were lost, but much of the future colony's supplies went down with it. Ayllón ordered a replacement vessel built on site—likely the earliest instance of European-style shipbuilding in what is now the United States.

The search for a viable settlement proved equally precarious. Pawleys Island offered poor soil and limited trade prospects. After reconnaissance missions, Ayllón moved roughly two hundred miles south to what the records describe as a "powerful river," probably near present-day Sapelo Sound, Georgia. In early September, the able-bodied men rode south on horseback, while others followed by sea. There, they began erecting houses and a church. On September 29, 1526—the feast day of Saint Michael—the settlement of San Miguel de Gualdape was formally established, the first European colony within the present-day United States.

It did not go well. Hunger, disease, internal conflict, and strained relations with local Native communities unraveled the enterprise almost immediately. On October 18, 1526, Ayllón died of an unspecified illness.[5] Then the colony fractured from within. A recorded uprising among enslaved Africans—one of the earliest documented in what would become the continental United States—shattered what little stability remained. By the end of two brutal months, San Miguel de Gualdape was abandoned.

Of the 600 to 700 who had departed that summer, only about 150 reached the Caribbean alive. Starvation, sickness, and rebellion had once again dissolved imperial intent. But, like earlier failures in Florida, it marked not a retreat from ambition but a rehearsal. The lesson Spain drew was not humility. If farming colonies failed, perhaps force would succeed.

1539 - De Soto Arrives

Hernando De Soto came to Florida with his sights set on a prize larger than the coastline. Back in Spain, tales of vast interior societies and possible riches had circulated like a contagion. De Soto, already wealthy from the Inca campaigns, secured authority to conquer and colonize "La Florida" and then assembled a rolling invasion meant to live off the land and keep moving.

Map, De Soto's Route, 1539-1542

In May 1539, he sailed from Havana with a fleet of nine vessels and landed on Florida's Gulf Coast. He intended to carve his way through the Southeast in search of gold and dominion comparable to what Cortés and Pizarro had achieved elsewhere. The expedition numbered more than six hundred soldiers, hundreds of African and Mexican slaves, and 24 priests. There were 220 horses, 300 hogs and dozens of Irish Wolfhounds. It was less a "party of explorers" than a mobile colony-in-arms, built for a multi-year campaign: to take, extract, and claim.

They landed near Tampa Bay, which was Tocobaga territory. His expedition's violence and extraction destabilized an already delicate balance of power, setting in motion consequences that would ripple outward long after his army had moved on.

For more than a year word had traveled ahead of De Soto's column, carried by traders, refugees, and the frightened survivors of villages that had watched the strangers arrive. They had crossed Florida and Georgia leaving behind a chain of violence: women were taken, and men killed or enslaved. They seized indigenous food stores, took hostages as guides, and imposed tribute on communities already navigating fragile political landscapes. Strange fevers had followed their path.

They plundered a mortuary temple where the dead had been laid after a pestilence destroyed their village. His men tore the pearls from the bodies—pounds of them—along with glass beads and metal tools buried beside the dead. The graves were stripped clean. From there the expedition moved north and west, dragging its prisoners with it.

Across the Carolinas and into the mountains of Tennessee, the column wandered in widening circles, plundering the storehouses of powerful chiefdoms. They spent a hundred days moving through wealthy territories, among them the domain of the Coosa confederacy. Horses trampled fields. Soldiers emptied granaries meant to feed entire towns through winter. De Soto and his band wintered in Apalachee territory near present-day Tallahassee. But the news had outrun them.

Across the Southeast, towns had begun to prepare. In October, near the lands of Tuscaloosa, thousands of warriors hid themselves inside houses and behind walls. When De Soto entered the town with a small guard, the trap closed. The fighting was savage and sudden. But the Spaniards survived, and responded with vengeance. Thousands were killed. The town burned until little remained but ash and charred timber.

The expedition moved west. In Mississippi and Arkansas, villages surrendered their stores of corn to the armed strangers resulting in widespread famine. In May of 1541 the Spaniards reached a river so wide it seemed like a moving sea—the Mississippi. They crossed it slowly on rafts and crude boats, pushing deeper into lands that had already heard the stories.

Some confederacies resisted.

Along the Arkansas River valley, during the brutal winter of 1541, the exhausted Spaniards struck the town of Anilco. Desperate and half starving, they rode in on horseback with the wolfhounds running beside them. Hundreds of people were slaughtered before the sun set.

Epidemics had begun with earlier coastal contact, but an armed column of hundreds, moving from chiefdom to chiefdom, accelerated transmission and destabilized alliances. Mortality rippled outward, and power structures shifted. Some communities vanished within a generation. The demographic and political map of the Southeast began to fracture under the combined weight of violence and contagion.

De Soto found no gold empire in Florida. He pressed westward. In the spring of 1542 he died of fever along the Mississippi. His men, unwilling to let the surrounding nations know their leader was gone, wrapped his body in blankets and sank it into the river under cover of darkness. By 1543, after four years and nearly four thousand miles of wandering, only about three hundred Spaniards staggered out of the interior and made their way back to Spanish territory, diminished and hollowed. Florida had not been conquered. It had been scarred.

❧

These early decades tell a clearer story than legend allows. Spain did not discover a paradise and build a city. It tested Florida three times over thirty years—first with settlers, then with a town, and finally with an army. Each effort exposed the same realities: organized Indigenous resistance, logistical fragility, unfamiliar ecology, and the high human cost of imposing empire on a densely inhabited landscape.

The frontier machine that would later define St. Augustine and Pensacola did not begin with stone forts. It began with failure.

Only after these collapses did Spain recalibrate—choosing in 1565 to build not an agricultural colony first, but a fortified port at St. Augustine. Not a farm, but a fortress. Florida itself had forced that decision. In doing so, it shaped how the empire would take root—not gently, not easily, but with walls, guns, and permanence carved from coquina stone.

The irony is stark. Spain claimed Florida decades before it could hold it. For half a century, Florida remained more aspiration than reality. It named the land long before it understood it and asserted sovereignty long before it controlled it.

But that early claim mattered. When France later attempted to establish a settlement at Fort Caroline, Spain responded with force. When Britain coveted Gulf ports, Spain invoked its prior rights. When the United States negotiated for the peninsula, it did so within a chain of legitimacy that began in 1513. A flag raised on a shoreline did not transform Florida overnight, but it changed the future arguments about who owned it. In 1513, with a name and a claim, Spain set the long contest for Florida in motion.

[1] Oviedo, Gonzalo Fernández de (1851). Historia general y natural de las Indias.
[2] Deagan, Kathleen A (1978). "Cultures in Transition: Fusion and Assimilation among the Eastern Timucua". In Milanich, Jerold T.; Proctor, Samuel (eds.). Tacachale: Essays on the Indians of Florida and Southeastern Georgia during the Historic Period. Gainesville, Florida: The University Presses of Florida.
[3] Milanich, Jerald T. (1998b). Florida Indians from Ancient Times to the Present. Gainesville, Florida: The University Press of Florida.
[4] Library of Congress, "Chi-Mobi: Writing Timucua in Seventeenth-Century Florida," Library of Congress Blogs – Worlds Revealed (Maps Blog), July 2021.
[5] Peck, Douglas T. (2001). "Lucas Vásquez de Ayllón's Doomed Colony of San Miguel de Gualdape". The Georgia Historical Quarterly.

2

The Birth of St. Augustine

Empire is born not in ceremony but in calculation.

— Anonymous

September 18, 1565. Twenty Miles North of St. Augustine

THE STORM HAD ALREADY killed men

Rain came sideways, driven by winds that bent the trees and flattened the marsh grass. The sky stayed iron-gray. For three days, the tempest had raged along the Florida coast, scattering ships and swallowing sound. Out at sea, vessels fought to survive. Inland, five hundred Spanish soldiers fought something less visible yet no less dangerous.

Mud.

They had been marching night and day—north from the new settlement of St. Augustine toward the French encampment at Fort Caroline—through terrain none of them understood. The maps were guesses, and the guides were uncertain. Water rose to their waists, then to their chests. Armor dragged them down. Powder had to be kept dry at all costs. Muskets were wrapped in oilcloth and prayer.

This was not a road. It was a swamp—thick with palmetto and cypress, alive with insects and reptiles the men had never seen. Snakes slipped through the reeds, and alligators broke the surface and disappeared. The ground gave way without warning. Every step had to be tested before weight was trusted.

By the second night, men began to fall behind. Fever. Exhaustion. Slipping beneath the water and not rising. One hundred men dropped out during the march—some lost, some left behind to recover if they could. No one stopped long enough to count.

At the head of the column, Pedro Menéndez de Avilés, soaked through and with boots rotting at the seams, pushed forward into a storm that should have turned them back. He understood what the French did not: the supply ships they were waiting for, full of reinforcements and soldiers, were still at sea, caught in the same hurricane. The French fort would be thinly defended.

The men behind him had not signed on for this. They had enlisted for land grants, wages, and advancement—some for faith, others for ambition. Few imagined wading chest-deep through black water in a foreign wilderness, marching toward an enemy who would show no mercy if the tide turned.

Somewhere ahead, through sheets of rain and darkness, lay a timber fort and a decision that would stain this coastline for centuries.

The storm did not break. They kept walking.

◆

Spring, 1565.

This story begins not in Florida but in the salt air of northern Spain, nine months earlier, in the port town of Avilés. Here, the harbor opened onto the Bay of Biscay — one of Europe's most unforgiving stretches of water. Storms rose quickly, and winds shifted without warning. If you survived here, you respected the ocean. One of those men was Pedro Menéndez de Avilés.

He was not born into royalty but into a life of daily labor and hard work. By his twenties, he was already commanding vessels, and by middle age, he had become one of Spain's most trusted naval officers. He hunted pirates, escorted treasure fleets, and, most surprisingly, spoke English — rare for a Spaniard of his class. He understood the movements of rival powers as well as he did tides and currents. At court, he was useful. At sea, he was indispensable.

In 1565, King Phillip II of Spain needed both.

The entire eastern seaboard of North America, what Spain called La Florida, had already been claimed in

Spain's name. The 1513 claim was old, and on paper it stretched north toward Nova Scotia, west to the Mississippi, and along the Gulf coast toward Texas. On maps, it looked secure, but in reality it was porous.

French Huguenots had recently established a foothold at Fort Caroline near present-day Jacksonville, while English privateers circled like wolves. The greatest artery of Spain's empire—the treasure fleets—sailed directly past this exposed coastline every year. Silver from Mexico, gold from Peru, chests of coins, and bars of metal, all pulled from the mountains of the Americas and loaded onto heavy galleons. These fleets gathered in Havana and then turned north, riding the powerful Gulf Stream through the Bahama Channel before striking east across the Atlantic toward Spain.

It was a narrow, dangerous passage. Ships ran aground on reefs, and hurricanes routinely scattered entire convoys. Survivors who staggered ashore along Florida's coast sometimes found themselves captives—absorbed into Indigenous societies, enslaved, or simply vanishing into a continent Europeans barely understood. Every wreck was not just a tragedy. It was a vulnerability.

From 1492 onward, Spain had probed the edge of this continent and planted its flags. Claims were declared, but Florida, with its low coastline edged with reefs and shoals, refused to cooperate.

Pedro Menéndez de Avilés

Men had come before. Juan Ponce de León in 1513,
then Pánfilo de Narváez in 1528, whose expedition
dissolved into starvation and shipwreck; Hernando de Soto
in 1539, who marched deep into the interior only to die
along the Mississippi River. There were more attempts—
royally sanctioned entradas meant to establish permanence.

None endured. Supplies ran thin, and supply ships missed their rendezvous. Men succumbed to hunger, fever, and conflict with Indigenous communities defending their homelands.

Florida was not Mexico. There were no visible cities of gold. The soil along much of the coast was sandy and stubborn, and crops refused to grow. Harbors were shallow, cluttered with sandbars that could gut a hull with a single miscalculation. The climate punished European assumptions, and the land swallowed ambition whole.

Empire, Faith, Ambition—and a Father's Hope.

By 1565, more than a dozen expeditions had failed to secure the peninsula. Florida had earned a reputation as Spain's graveyard. King Philip II did not need another explorer. He needed a man who could establish a permanent military harbor, eliminate French intrusion, and anchor Spain's claim in timber, stone, and blood, if necessary.

He chose Menéndez.

For Menéndez, there was the promise of royal favor and land grants. There was the opportunity to secure Spain's treasure fleets and elevate his family's standing for generations. There was the missionary mandate—to expand Catholic dominion against Protestant encroachment. And there was something more personal: his son, Juan, had vanished years earlier in these waters after a shipwreck off the Florida coast. Menéndez believed

Juan might still be alive, perhaps living among Indigenous communities.

The commission was clear: sail to Florida, eliminate the French threat, and establish a settlement strong enough to protect the treasure fleets. This would not be a trading post or a seasonal camp. It would be a city.

❖

When Menéndez's fleet of 800 people gathered at Cádiz in 1565, roughly 50 Africans joined them—some free, others enslaved. Some came from Seville's narrow streets, where the smell of the Guadalquivir mingled with tar and spice, and where Black men carried cargo along the docks and Black women stood in parish lines beneath vaulted stone.

Spain in the 15th–16th centuries had a visible African and Afro-Iberian population, especially in port and commercial cities tied to Atlantic trade. Enslavement in Iberia was real and widespread, including in Seville. At the same time, Iberian slavery was not a single, uniform condition. Manumission existed and produced free Black communities, often Catholic, Spanish-speaking, and embedded in urban life.

Some of the Africans who boarded Menéndez's ships that day had crossed the Atlantic in chains years earlier, arriving in Spain enslaved; others had been born under its bells, baptized with Spanish names, and spoke Castilian as their first language. Freedom and bondage lived side by side in that city, sometimes within the same household.

They came not as an afterthought but as part of the machinery and the human mix that kept Spain's Atlantic empire running. Some were property and would be put to work immediately on the blunt necessities of survival: timber, trenches, and the first hard edges of a fort in a wet, unfamiliar world. Others were free Black Catholics whose freedom had been purchased or granted, yet was always precarious.

They took the journey for reasons not unlike the Spanish, Germans, or others seeking opportunity. At least those who could choose. Florida promised nothing certain, but it also offered distance from crowded hierarchies at home. The colony would need hands and muscle. It would need men and women of faith.

The Africans who would step onto the beach in St. Augustine would be woven into the colonial structure from day one, praying in the same parish and living under laws that could confine them and, at times, release them. They were there not as a single story but as several: owned and unowned, recent arrivals and second-generation Iberians, men and women who had already learned to navigate a world that labeled them yet depended on them.

The Fleet

Menéndez's fleet of nineteen ships left Spain in the summer of 1565, but storms and delays thinned their number before they ever reached the open Atlantic. By the time the armada cleared the Canary Islands and pushed westward, less than a dozen vessels remained.[1]

They carried 1,500 souls: soldiers hardened by European wars and sailors from Asturias and Andalusia. They were tailors, hatmakers, surgeons, barbers, and even beer brewers. There were 26 families. They were Spanish, Portuguese, English, French, Flemish, German, and African. Seven Franciscan clergy would plant the cross as firmly as the soldiers planted the banner.

Illustration, Spanish Ship c 1560

These were not settlers in the New England sense. They were instruments of policy. Artillery pieces, horses, seed grain, timber tools, and portable altars filled the holds. The fleet carried livestock and iron hardware, along with barrels of biscuit and salted meat—enough to found not a camp but a fortified town. Spain was not experimenting. It was committing.

The crossing itself took roughly two months. The Atlantic was rarely obedient. Hurricanes churned in late summer, and Menéndez's ships encountered violent storms that scattered the fleet and forced repairs at sea. One vessel foundered. Others limped westward under torn canvas. Halfway across the ocean, all but 5 of his ships were lost, including the supply ship carrying everything they would need to survive.

When the remaining ships finally sighted the Florida coast in late August 1565, they had already been tested by water and wind before ever facing French rivals or unfamiliar shores. The people who stepped onto the sands near what would become St. Augustine had already endured a trial. The city they were about to found was born of calculation, attrition, and the stubborn refusal of an empire to yield its claim.

St. Augustine

On September 8, 1565, Menéndez finally came ashore on Florida's northeastern coast and named the settlement St. Augustine, honoring the feast day of Saint Augustine, on which his ships had first sighted land. They waved Spanish flags and fired cannons. There was pageantry and blessings, and according to Priest Father Lopez, they were not alone. Indigenous people were watching. After witnessing the spectacle with curiosity, they, too, joined the Spaniards in kissing the cross and the flag.

Illustration, Spanish and Timucua meet at Seloy

A meal was prepared for everyone, including the Native people. Garbanzo beans, salted meats, and olive oil were served at our country's first Thanksgiving.

This was the beginning of a strategic empire in North America—a fortified response to rivals and the violent uncertainty of the Atlantic world. It was not founded by pilgrims seeking liberty. It was founded by a naval commander carrying out orders. From that decision—

rooted in silver, seawater, and Spain's fear of losing both—
America's oldest European city was born.

————————————❖————————————

Seloy, September 8, 1565

The people of Seloy watched the strangers come ashore in
armor that caught the sun. They watched them kneel and
raise a cross. They listened to the unfamiliar cadence of
prayer drifting over the dunes. The ships, floating
fortresses of timber and canvas, sat just beyond the
breakers, heavy with men who had crossed an ocean to
stand here.

This was Timucua land. And the Timucua chief at Seloy,
what is today St. Augustine, faced a calculation.

He had seen strangers before. Spanish expeditions had
come and gone for decades—sometimes trading,
sometimes demanding food, and often leaving sickness in
their wake. But these newcomers were different. They had
brought women and livestock and had begun unloading
supplies as if they intended to stay.

Why welcome them at all? Because the world of 1565
was already becoming unstable. Spain's entry into Florida
wasn't a "first contact" moment. It was a slow-moving
catastrophe. As expeditions probed the coastline and
pushed inland, Columbus, de Soto, and others brought a
new kind of violence through old political landscapes.
They took food and captives to serve as guides. They

demanded allegiance from chiefs who had their own rivals, obligations, and reasons to say yes or no. Even when an expedition moved on, it didn't leave the world unchanged.

It left grief, fear, and disease—the invisible stowaway that traveled faster than any horse. The epidemics had thinned populations and unsettled alliances. Now rival chiefdoms were maneuvering for advantage.

When French Huguenots under René Goulaine de Laudonnière built Fort Caroline in 1564, they did so within Saturiwa territory. The resulting alliance between the newcomers and the Saturiwa was pragmatic. The French served as useful counterweights to Spanish ambition: new trade partners and another lever in a political landscape already defined by rivalry. The Timucua, therefore, were not choosing between peace and conflict. They were choosing between competing foreigners.

Welcoming Pedro Menéndez de Avilés into Seloy was not surrender. It was strategy. The Spanish needed food, shelter, and local knowledge. The Timucua needed allies— steel weapons, military support, and leverage against rivals. On that September day, accommodation made sense. The Spanish were permitted to occupy the village. Houses were shared, and fields were planted.

It was a cautious, but promising start.

Fort Caroline

But there was a problem. In 1564, France had carved out a foothold along the very coastline Spain claimed as its own.

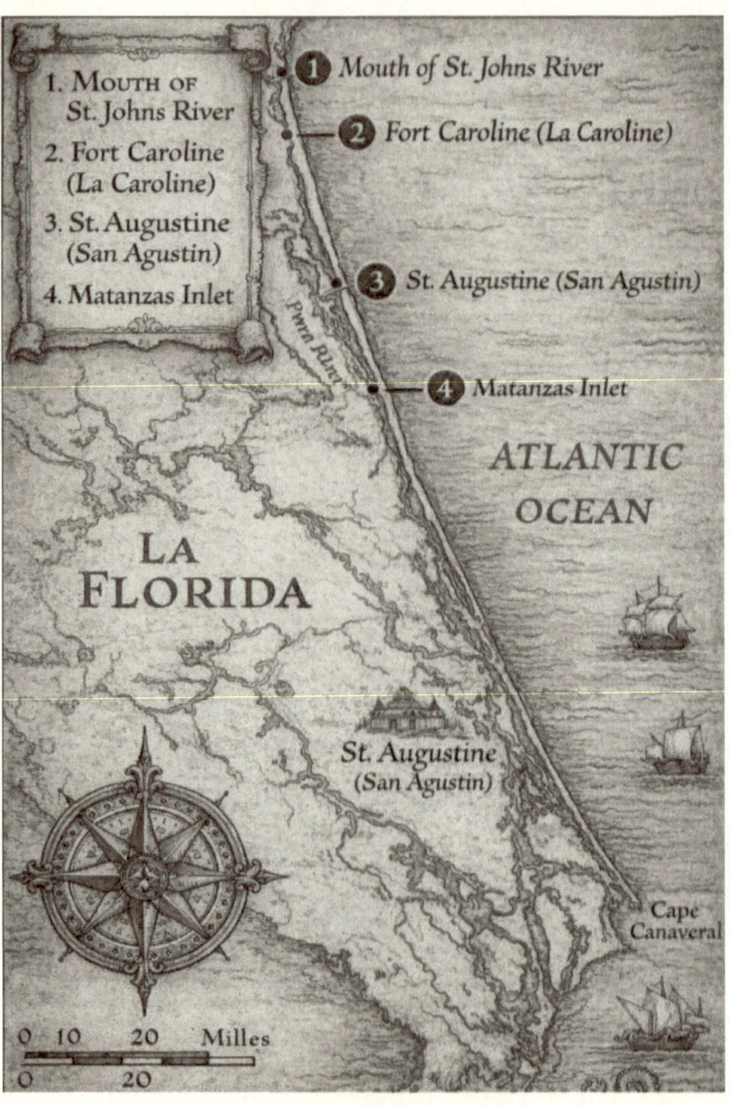

Map of Florida Coast, 1565

French Huguenots had built Fort Caroline along the St. Johns River near present-day Jacksonville, a timber fort in the middle of Spanish-claimed La Florida. To Madrid, it was more than trespass. It was heresy planted within imperial territory. Protestant settlers occupied a corridor through which Spain's treasure fleets sailed. It would not be allowed.

On paper, France had no right to be there. Diplomatic agreements among Catholic crowns had recognized Spain's claims in the Atlantic. But paper meant little on a continent still measured in timber and presence. The French were desperate—short on food, wracked by illness, and dependent on fragile alliances with local Indigenous groups. Their colony was clinging to survival. Supply ships had been dispatched from France, and if those reinforcements arrived first, the foothold might become permanent.

Menéndez understood the timing. The mission from settlement to combat shifted. This would not simply be a founding, but a military campaign. King Philip II of Spain was explicit: the French must be removed by any means necessary.[2] Spain would not tolerate a rival power on the flank of its treasure route.

The French, however, had no intention of abandoning their post. They had muskets, artillery, and just enough hope to fight. In raw numbers, the forces were not wildly unequal. Both sides were thinly supplied, far from home, and dependent on the sea. The difference would not be manpower alone but timing, weather, and luck.

September 20, 1565

Determined to strike the new Spanish position before it hardened, French Commander Jean Ribault sailed south with much of his force, intending to attack St. Augustine directly. The hurricane that had battered Menéndez's march now turned on the French fleet. Ships were driven off course, smashed against shoals, and wrecked along the coast near present-day Daytona Beach. Survivors staggered ashore, scattered and exhausted.

The balance shifted in a single storm.

With the French fleet disabled and their fort thinly defended, Pedro Menéndez de Avilés and his exhausted men finally arrived at Fort Caroline just before dawn on September 20.

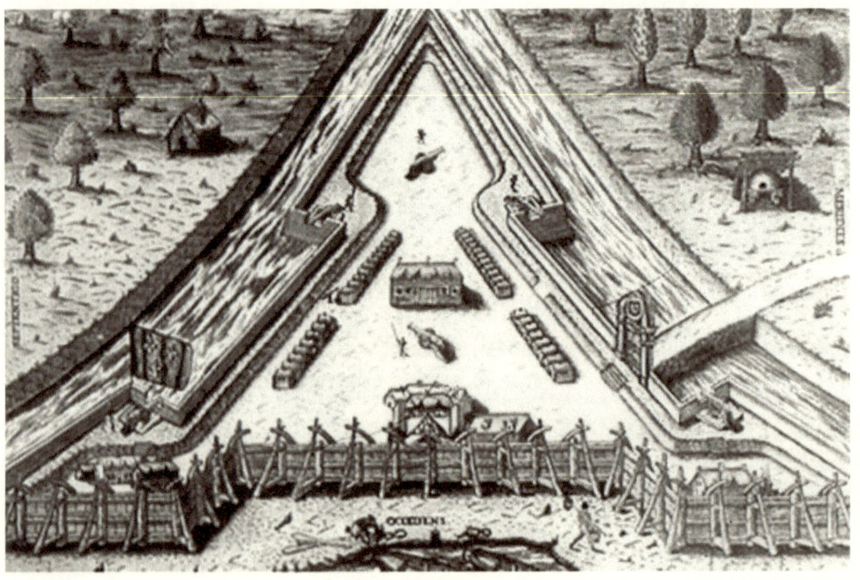

Fort Caroline

The French inside were caught completely unprepared. At first light, the Spanish surged over the walls. The fighting was brief and brutal. Most of the French soldiers and officers—nearly four hundred—were killed. A small number of skilled artisans were spared, and women and children were taken captive. The fort was stripped. Lutheran religious texts were seized. Weapons, coins, and goods were cataloged as spoils, and the Spanish renamed the stronghold San Mateo, marking the day of its capture on the feast of Saint Matthew.

Within days, the Spanish returned to St. Augustine, victorious yet hardened. The conflict was not entirely over—French shipwreck survivors would soon face their own grim fate farther south at what would later be called Matanzas, "slaughters." But the decisive blow had been struck. In less than two weeks, Spain had founded a city and eliminated its primary rival along Florida's coast.

St. Augustine survived because of timing, weather, and a willingness to use violence without hesitation.

The ground still remembers.

Archaeologists working along the banks of the St. Johns River, near the site long associated with Fort Caroline, have uncovered physical traces of that violent September. Post molds and structural remains suggest the footprint of a European-style fortification. A stone pillar—similar to those depicted in early engravings—has been documented along the coastal margins tied to the sixteenth-century occupation. The soil itself holds the outline of empire.

Farther south, in and around St. Augustine, excavations just north of the present-day downtown core have uncovered evidence of the earliest Spanish settlement layers. Archaeologists have unearthed European-style wells—circular shafts lined and reinforced in ways unfamiliar to Indigenous building traditions. Glass trade beads, fragments of olive jars, iron hardware, medicine vials, ceramics, and devotional objects have surfaced beneath streets now paved with asphalt and crowded with tourist foot traffic.[3]

These are not romantic relics. They are practical things—containers, tools, personal effects—the debris of survival. They confirm what documents alone can only suggest: that people stayed. They stored water, treated illness, and built a settlement according to European patterns while living within an Indigenous landscape.

Illustration of St. Augustine, early 1600s

What makes these finds powerful is their location. The earliest material evidence of St. Augustine does not fit neatly within the later colonial street grid. It lies slightly north of the modern historic district, suggesting that the first encampment shifted before stabilizing. The city we walk in today is not exactly where it began.

Paper records tell us that Menéndez founded a town. The artifacts show how fragile that beginning was — temporary wells, hurried construction, and improvised defenses. Empire did not arrive in stone but in wood, glass, iron, and effort buried in unstable soil.

Five centuries later, the spade continues to confirm what the chronicles described: this was no mythic landing. It was a working settlement, etched into the earth, posthole by posthole.

Doña Antonia, Colonial Pawn

On Florida's southwest coast, far from the sandy inlet of St. Augustine, power wore a different face. The Calusa chief, whom the Spanish called King Carlos, commanded tribute and obedience in a world shaped by tide and canoe. When Pedro Menéndez de Avilés came south to consolidate Spain's claim, he did not arrive among the helpless. He arrived in a kingdom.

Calusa diplomacy had its own grammar. If you wished to secure peace on a frontier, you exchanged something tangible. Carlos offered his sister. Her Calusa name is lost to us, but the Spanish recorded her baptismal name instead: Doña Antonia.

Menéndez protested; after all, he already had a wife in Spain. But in a place where alliances are fragile and supply lines thin, "wife" meant more than companionship. It meant treaty and mutual obligation. It also meant that the Spanish governor and the Calusa chief would now share blood, at least symbolically.

So he accepted. Antonia was sent to Havana to be instructed in the Catholic faith. In Spanish eyes, this religious instruction was the salvation of a soul. But

Antonia did not behave like a clause in a contract. When Menéndez brokered a peace that was unfavorable to the Calusa in dealings with the Tocobaga, her anger surfaced. She objected and spoke out. Carlos now wanted his sister returned. Back and forth, Antonia moved—Florida to Havana, Havana to Florida—as relations improved, then soured. She became the human pawn on which policy turned. Not silent or passive, but constrained within a structure built by men who believed they controlled the board.

By 1568, diplomacy had collapsed into violence. Tensions between the Calusa and the Spanish escalated, and King Carlos was killed by Spanish soldiers. The experiment in marital alliance ended as so many early Florida arrangements did—with blood in the water.

Antonia remained among her people for a time, teaching Catholic practice in a land where belief and politics had become inseparable. Later, she returned to Havana, where she died, far from the mangrove kingdom that had first defined her.

It was a pattern that repeated: in Spanish Florida, diplomacy often ran through women's bodies—marriage as treaty, baptism as bond, relocation as control. But women were not inert vessels of policy. They carried memory, outrage, and influence. The founding of St. Augustine was not only a story of ships and forts but also a beginning rooted in human bargaining, where empire pressed its terms into flesh—and sometimes met resistance.

Later English colonies often tried to separate and classify, whereas Spanish Florida—messy, Catholic, improvised—integrated out of necessity. And women are where that integration is most visible, most human, and most undeniable.

The Timucua

As St. Augustine took root, the balance of power between the newcomers and the Timucua shifted. What began as alliance hardened into expectation. Tribute became labor, and religious instruction became a new obligation. Spanish permanence narrowed Timucua autonomy in ways the first meeting on the shore could not fully predict.

From the beginning, the city's survival depended as much on them as on any fleet that crossed the Atlantic. The

Timucua did not disappear when the Spanish arrived. They negotiated, adapted, and they endured. But the early alliance did not last.

Within months of the founding, Pedro Menéndez left St. Augustine to consolidate Spain's hold elsewhere along the coast and in the Caribbean. He left behind a fragile outpost of unfinished fortifications, limited stores, and a garrison dependent on local food supplies. What had felt like momentum in September hardened into scarcity by winter.

Athore, son of the Timucuan chief Saturiwa, showing René Laudonnière a monument placed by Jean Ribault.

Rations thinned quickly. The Spanish had assumed resupply would come regularly from Havana and Spain, but storms delayed ships and bureaucracy slowed departures. Hunger sharpened tempers. Soldiers accustomed to European campaigns now found themselves

58

in a subtropical landscape that resisted their farming methods. Crops failed, salted meat spoiled, and men grew sick.

The strain altered the relationship with the Timucua.

Accommodation began to fray under pressure. Indigenous leaders, facing their own resource limits and wary of the settlement's growing permanence, reassessed the bargain. The newcomers were no longer temporary allies against the French; they were a fixed presence, reshaping land and authority.

Raids began. Timucua warriors first attacked Spanish foraging parties. Supplies disappeared along woodland paths, and tension turned to open hostility. At one point in the colony's earliest months, the settlement itself was attacked and burned. Structures of timber and thatch offered little resistance to fire. Smoke rose over the palmettos, and the Spanish found themselves exposed — hungry, outnumbered, and without their commander.

St. Augustine nearly ended before it began.[4]

When Menéndez returned after roughly four months away, he returned to instability. If the birth of the city was violent, its infancy was precarious.

The relationship with native tribes did not turn from fire to friendship overnight. After the first effort to expel the newcomers, the relationship between the colony and the surrounding Timucua settled into something more complicated than open war and far less stable than peace.

Menéndez realized the settlement was too exposed, too dependent, and too easily set alight. Within a year of its founding, the Spanish moved to more defensible ground, fortifying their camp and reorganizing their lives around the expectation of attack. Wood replaced thatch, and watchfulness replaced ceremony. The early dream of easy coexistence had burned with the first structures.

But constant warfare serves no one for long.

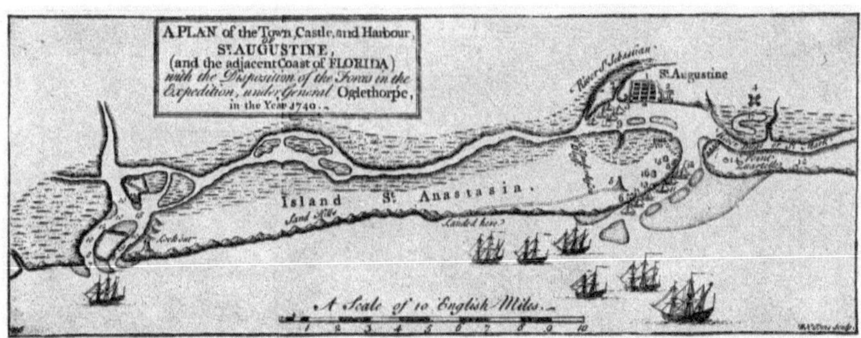

Map of St. Augustine

The Spanish could not feed themselves without the Native food systems of maize, fish, deer, and gathered plants. The Timucua could not ignore the reality that these foreigners possessed steel, firearms, and access to distant power. So the violence ebbed and flowed. A truce here, a trade there, a raid in response to overreach, and a warning delivered in the night. It was frontier diplomacy—measured in hunger, leverage, and memory.

Over the next decade, St. Augustine began to take on the shape of a town rather than a military encampment. A central plaza was laid out—an open square that served as

60

the civic heart, parade ground, marketplace, and stage for proclamations. Festivals marked feast days, and processions wound through sandy streets. Soldiers drilled, while merchants and traders bartered goods from Havana, Spain, and nearby Indigenous communities. The rhythms of ordinary life began to overlay the memory of violence.

A parish church rose near the plaza—the earliest Catholic parish established in what would become the continental United States. Its bell tower stood visible to ships approaching the inlet, a signal as practical as it was spiritual. It told incoming sailors that this was no longer a temporary claim staked in sand. It was a community with ritual, hierarchy, and permanence.

Illustration, Parish Church in Saint Augustine

Menéndez himself returned to Spain in 1574. He died that same year, honored by the Crown but far from the coastline he had fought to secure. His son, lost years earlier in a Florida shipwreck, was never found. The founding of America's oldest European city had been driven in part by a father's hope; it ended without reunion.

Women in Early Spanish Florida

Women and children rarely dominate the chronicles of conquest. But they appear where permanence begins—parish records, baptismal entries, marriage dispensations, and letters sent back to Spain describing illness, births, fear, and small triumphs. The domestic archive tells a different story from the battlefield. It shows cooking fires shared, gardens planted, and language learned across kinship lines. It was their daily work, after all, that kept the fragile frontier settlements from collapsing back into the wilderness.

Long before Europeans arrived, Timucuan women were the backbone of an agricultural society. They raised staple crops—corn, beans, squash, pumpkins, and melons—managed household production, cooked, cleaned, and turned animal hides into clothing. They made pottery for storage and cooking—technologies so ordinary we overlook them, even though they make a sedentary life possible.

Villages were not "primitive." They were organized labor systems sustained by women's expertise and seasonal knowledge. Women were the stewards of continuity, and in many Indigenous societies of the Southeast, kinship was matrilineal—tracing descent, property rights, and social status through the mother's line. This placed women at the heart of cultural preservation. They maintained oral histories, upheld ritual practices, and served as healers and midwives. With an intimate understanding of the land, they knew what to plant, when to gather, how to treat illness, and how to sustain life in an environment where survival required harmony, not conquest.

Then came the violence that male chronicles often describe as exploration.

When Hernando de Soto marched through Florida in 1539 with an army of more than five hundred men, it was a moving act of extraction. Women were taken to serve as consorts and captives. This was not incidental, but strategic: control the women, and you control the social fabric.

Brides of the Borderland

While history remembers the governors and the battles, it often forgets the weddings. In the decades leading up to the turn of the 17th century, St. Augustine soldiers did what frontier soldiers have always done: they rooted themselves where they stood. Marriage records show that roughly a quarter of documented unions joined Spanish settlers with Native women.[5] These were not rare exceptions, but a pattern. Alliances moved from treaty to household.

From those households came children. The first recorded children of European descent born on what is now American soil were born here, decades before Jamestown. In 1566, Martín de Argüelles Jr. was entered in the parish register of St. Augustine.[6] He would not have known he was a milestone. He was simply a child in a town trying to survive.

Another early record survives. The ink is steady, and the language is formal and routine. But the details carry weight.

Nearly 35 years after the colonists arrived, Father Richard Arthur entered a marriage into the parish book of St. Augustine: Agustín and Francisca. Francisca is described as "negra of Doña Petronilla." The phrase is matter-of-fact. It tells us she is Black. It tells us she belongs to a household and that the colony's first generation had already sorted people into ranks.

Then come the sponsors: Simón and María, also Black.

That's the part historians pause over. Sponsors were not random names. In a frontier town of a few hundred souls, they were chosen witnesses—people who stood as moral guarantors, sometimes as extended family. Their presence tells us there was already a Black community substantial enough to provide its own spiritual kinship network. Not isolated individuals, but a web.[7]

The document does not tell us whether Agustín was free or enslaved. It does not tell us whether Francisca would ever purchase her freedom, inherit it, or remain in bondage. The record doesn't editorialize, it simply fixes them in place—two people standing before an altar in the oldest European town in what would become the United States.

Illustration, Spanish Woman

By the end of the sixteenth century, Africans in St. Augustine were not just laboring on palisades or hauling stone. They were marrying and building families under Spanish law and Catholic ritual.

It is a small entry, but it tells us something bigger. Forty-two years before Jamestown, families were already growing in Florida. Children played in sandy streets near the plaza. Indigenous and Spanish worlds met not only in councils and skirmishes but also in kitchens and cradles. Collaboration was practical: shared labor in the fields, exchange of foodways, and adaptation to the climate. Cultural lines blurred long before English colonies would attempt to harden them.

St. Augustine had become a town where men vastly outnumbered women, and survival depended on informal economies—fishing, carpentry, barter, and side trades. Soldiers were required to live in comrade groups to pool rations. "Private life" was often communal. Francisco Camacho, who arrived in Saint Augustine sometime in the 1560s from Cádiz, married a Native woman named Teresa.

In 1580, their household included Francisco, Teresa, Teresa's sister Catalina, and Catalina's son Juan.[8] That snapshot shows kin networks crossing cultures and women anchoring extended households. Fewer than half of the Spanish men were married, and among those who were, not all had Spanish wives. The frontier married locally. When men died—as they often did—women became infrastructure.

Francisca de Vera

Francisca de Vera, widowed sometime in the 1570s, supported herself by turning her home into a boardinghouse, renting space to soldiers. Those soldiers worked side jobs, such as carpentry or barbering, to supplement thin wages. Francisca's story is not dramatic, but it is essential: she represents the female economy that made garrisons livable. A colony can survive raids and hurricanes. It can't survive without food, washing, shelter, and someone to keep accounts.

By 1580, Spain's grand design had narrowed to two fragile anchors. Of the thirteen forts and settlements established along the Atlantic corridor, only two endured: St. Augustine and Santa Elena, nearly 220 miles to the north on present-day Parris Island. The rest—outposts carved into marsh and pine forest—had withered from distance, disease, Indigenous resistance, supply failures, and the sheer cost of empire.

The map had shrunk. Florida was no longer just a rumor to be tested but a strategic corridor to defend. To make it viable, Spain needed food, labor, and allies. North Florida's Indigenous nations—especially the Timucua and Apalachee—became central to that plan.

By 1580, St. Augustine had not yet become secure, but it had become stubborn. What survived was not conquest, but endurance.

[1] Scott Weidensaul (2012). The First Frontier: The Forgotten History of Struggle, Savagery, and Endurance in Early America. Houghton Mifflin Harcourt.

[2] Michael Kenny (1934). The Romance of the Floridas: The Finding and the Founding.

[3] Jerald T. Milanich and Kathleen A. Deagan, The Fountain of Youth Park (FOY) Site (8SJ31): 1999–2000 Field Season Report, Florida Museum of Natural History, University of Florida, 2000.

[4] Crutchfield, James A.; Moutlon, Candy; Terry Del Bene (March 26, 2015). The Settlement of America: An Encyclopedia of Westward Expansion from Jamestown to the Closing of the Frontier. Routledge.

[5] Kathleen A. Deagan, "Mestizaje in Colonial St. Augustine," Ethnohistory 20, no. 1 (1973).

[6] University of Florida George A. Smathers Libraries, "Colonial Florida Parish Records," Colonial Florida Research Guide.

[7] Catholic Archdiocese of St. Augustine, Marriage record for "Augustin and Francisca," 1598 (sacramental register entry; reproduced as "First Known Black Marriage Record").

[8] Amy Turner Bushnell, Situado and Sabana: Spain's Support System for the Presidio and Mission Provinces of Florida (Athens: University of Georgia Press, 1994).

3

Greed, Gold and God: 1580-1675

Government organizes the conquest, and religion justifies it.

—Jared Diamond

Conquest by Gospel

The bells did not ring for worship alone. They rang to gather bodies.

In the long, humid mornings of northern Florida, the sound carried over hammocks and pine trees, across fields that had once belonged to clan and kin. It called people into squares laid out by strangers—timber churches rising where council houses once stood, crosses planted in soil that had known other sacred fires.

By the late sixteenth century, Spain had learned that forts alone were not enough. Soldiers could hold a harbor, but not a continent. What held a frontier were people—fed, baptized, and counted. So the Franciscans came.

From the harbors and coasts outward through Timucua towns and along the corridors toward what is now Georgia, they built a chain of missions: San Juan, San Pedro, San Luis. Each one a node in a tightening net. The architecture was simple—chapel, convento, storehouse, fields—but the design was strategic. Draw dispersed villages into central places and replace clan authority with sacrament. Turn hunters and farmers into laborers in an imperial system that ultimately ran across the Atlantic to Spain.

After de Soto's disastrous expedition forty years earlier, Charles V (King Carlos V of Spain) issued new directives calling for more humane treatment of Indigenous peoples than had been permitted in earlier explorations. The Crown had already debated the morality of conquest, as the brutality of early campaigns had sparked a theological crisis in Spain itself.

Indigenous peoples were to be regarded as vassals of the Crown—not as chattel. They were to be converted, taxed, and organized—but not legally enslaved as a class. On paper, Native people were to be treated as subjects equal before the law, even if social hierarchy remained real. The rhetoric shifted from conquest by sword to conquest by gospel.

By the late 1500s, the mission system spanned northern Florida and extended into present-day Georgia. Indigenous leaders were courted through gift exchange—cloth, tools, livestock, and ritual objects—building networks of reciprocity. Conversion was spiritual, but it was also diplomatic. A baptized chief was a political ally.

Conversion was true for some. They found meaning in the new rituals, folded saints into older cosmologies, and learned prayers in a language not their own. But belief was not the only currency in this exchange. Demographic collapse had altered everything.

Map of Spanish Missions in Florida 1565-1763

Disease arrived in waves: measles, smallpox, influenza, and other epidemics spread along mission corridors, trade routes, and in the concentrated villages. Populations dropped, and leadership lines broke. Whole communities were forced to reorganize or merge, and the politics of north Florida shifted under their feet. Towns were hollowed out, and leadership fractured. By the time Spain's mission system reached deeply into these regions, it was not entering static societies but communities already reshaped by war, epidemic, displacement, and the long shadow of first contact.

In that landscape, a mission was more than a church. It offered a promise of Spanish steel in moments of danger and rations during a lean season. It offered a fragile shield against annihilation. Traditional authority didn't simply vanish. Chiefs and local leaders often adapted, negotiated, and resisted, but over time, pressure, disease, and shifting power forced accommodation. Some entered willingly; others out of necessity. Most did so under pressure. Stone by stone, the mission world steadily tilted power toward this new Spanish system. Across Florida, the result was not "cultural change." It was demographic collapse and political reordering.

In the 1590s, missionaries entered Potano territory, and by 1633, five missions had been established there. Beginning in 1597, Spanish missionaries worked steadily among the Mocama and Yustaga, and colonial authorities formalized their territories as the Timucua Province. Over time, smaller neighboring provinces were folded into this administrative unit, increasing the Northern Utina's nominal prominence within the mission system.

The Saturiwa were drawn in, and Mission San Juan del Puerto was established at their main village. There, the Franciscan friar Francisco Pareja later studied and documented the Timucua language in remarkable detail. By the end of the sixteenth century, the Utina confederacy had fractured, and nearly all of the known Eastern Timucua chiefdoms were gradually drawn into it as well. What had once been a dense, competitive political landscape of multiple dialects, rival chiefs, and fluid alliances began to thin. The indigenous world did not vanish overnight. It narrowed.

As it narrowed, Spanish missions advanced into the spaces left behind—not into empty land, but into communities struggling to reorganize after catastrophe. Mission towns reorganized settlement patterns, consolidated dispersed villages, and tied them—spiritually and economically—to St. Augustine.

Our Lady of La Leche Mission, Florida

The empire called it salvation. The friars called it souls. The governors called it order. But for the native people who moved into those mission towns, it was something more complicated: a calculation made under pressure, a decision shaped by grief, fear, and the narrowing options in a world remade by invasion.

The Timucua paid the heaviest price. Within a generation of sustained European contact, their world contracted with terrifying speed. Leaders died. Elders died. Children died. Social memory thinned. By some estimates, within roughly twenty years of intensified contact, Timucua populations in parts of north Florida had declined by as much as seventy-five percent.[1] War compounded the losses—skirmishes with the Spanish, conflicts with rival Indigenous groups destabilized by the same pressures, and raids triggered by shifting alliances.

A chiefdom built on tribute and kinship cannot function the same way when three out of four people are gone. Fields go unplanted, and traditional spiritual ceremonies cannot be properly held. Authority fractures when hereditary lines are interrupted by disease. The Spanish did not need to conquer every town by force; epidemic disease did what armies could not.

Demography is destiny. By the time Britain acquired Florida in 1763, only a small remnant of the Timucua remained—perhaps around 125 people according to Spanish records.[2]

Yet accommodation did not erase resentment. Like other Western Timucua groups, the Potano would later participate in the Timucua Rebellion of 1656—a last, desperate assertion of autonomy. When the revolt was crushed, their society suffered a catastrophic decline.

The bells kept ringing.

❖

Florida, May 29, 1586

They saw the sails before they heard the guns. Twenty-five years after its founding, St. Augustine no longer looked like a desperate encampment. There were shops near the plaza, taverns, and a parish church stood in the square, its bell audible over the marsh. Children ran through corridors, and fishermen brought their catch upriver. It was still small, still vulnerable—but it was alive.

Then, one summer morning in 1586, the horizon filled.

Twenty-three warships rode the Atlantic swell—dark hulls bristling with cannon. Nearly two thousand armed men stood ready aboard them. At their head was Francis Drake.

To the English, he was a hero of the seas. To Spain, he was something else entirely: El Draque—the Dragon. A raider, a Protestant scourge, a man who turned Catholic shipping lanes into hunting grounds. He sailed not only for plunder but also for humiliation, carrying Queen Elizabeth's commission in one hand and personal fury in the other. What he did not seize, he burned. What he could not carry, he destroyed.

The Spanish in St. Augustine understood the danger immediately. They were outmanned, outgunned, and outranged. The town had no stone fortress yet—only wooden defenses and courage stretched thin. When Drake's fleet anchored offshore and his landing parties advanced, residents fled inland with what they could carry. Families vanished into hammocks and pinewoods. Livestock were abandoned, doors left swinging.

Illustration, Sir Francis Drake and Queen Elizabeth I

Only eighty soldiers remained behind. They gathered the treasury chest, the small, heavy symbol of imperial order, and retreated to the fort. It was not enough. Drake's men came ashore in force, drums beating, and banners snapping. English boots struck Spanish sand.

To Drake, St. Augustine was not an innocent town but a rival foothold in a widening Atlantic contest. England was attempting to establish its own colony at Roanoke, while Spanish Florida posed a threat to Protestant ambitions and competition with Catholic expansion. Drake himself had reason to despise Spain. Years earlier, Spanish forces had attacked English shipping and commerce. He answered insult with fire.

Men of God had built this town. Missionaries and soldiers had planted it in faith and ambition. Now, a man of greed, at least in Spanish eyes, would test whether it could survive the age of empires.

By nightfall, St. Augustine was in ashes.[3]

A Collision of Empires

Drake had not appeared in St. Augustine by accident. He arrived as the sharp edge of English policy.

Spain under Philip II was not merely another European kingdom. It was the era's superpower—rich in American silver, dominant in the Caribbean, and strung across the oceans by a logistics network of treasure fleets, fortified ports, and Catholic authority. Spanish possessions and claims stretched from Mexico and Peru to the islands of the Caribbean, from the Philippines to the Atlantic coast of North America. Spain's money bought soldiers, its ships carried cannon, and its faith carried a mandate: defend Catholic Europe and contain Protestant rivals.

England, meanwhile, was the scrappy challenger. Under Elizabeth I, it was Protestant, smaller, and increasingly boxed in—shut out of Spain's imperial monopoly and watching Spanish wealth fund wars and influence across Europe. The 1580s were a decade of escalation: England supported Dutch rebels fighting Spain in the Netherlands; Catholic conspiracies and assassination fears churned in London; commerce and religion braided together into something combustible. In that atmosphere, "trade" and "war" were often the same thing, with different paperwork.

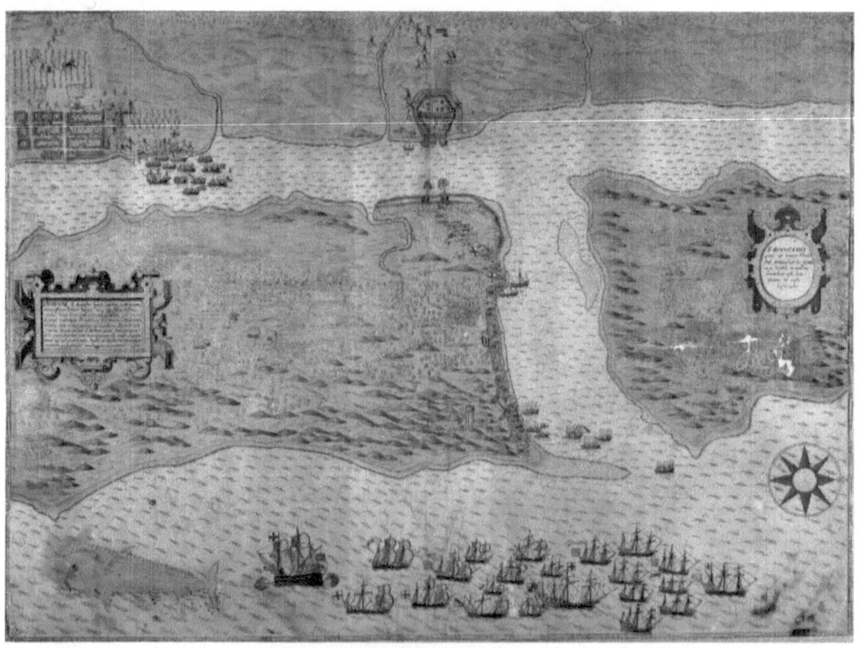

Baptista Boazio's Map of Sir Francis Drake's Raid on St. Augustine (published in 1589). Public Domain.

So, Elizabeth did what weaker sea powers have always done against stronger empires: she outsourced violence.

She issued commissions—licenses that turned piracy into strategy. Privateers could raid Spanish shipping, sack Spanish ports, and cripple Spain's wealth pipeline, all while giving the Crown plausible deniability. It was state-sponsored theft cloaked in patriotism. And no one was better at it than Sir Francis Drake.

Drake had already made his name in Spanish blood and silver. He had raided Caribbean ports, struck at the treasure routes, and circumnavigated the globe—returning not only rich but also mythic. To the English, he was daring personified: a sailor who embarrassed the largest empire on earth. To the Spanish, he was not a rival officer but a criminal with royal protection, a Protestant terror who burned towns and mocked the cross. And he was Queen Elizabeth I's chosen weapon.

In 1585, England effectively unleashed him on Spain's Atlantic world. Drake sailed west with a large force and began tearing at Spain's perimeter—seizing ports, capturing ships, and making a terrifying point: Spain's empire was vast, but it could be hurt. His campaign swept through the Caribbean like a fever. When he turned north toward Florida, St. Augustine came into view as exactly what it was: a small, exposed Spanish foothold guarding the sea-lane corridor and anchoring Spain's claim on the Atlantic coast.

That is why St. Augustine became a target, not for its gold but for its position. It sat at the edge of the currents and shipping routes; it was a Catholic outpost in a contest increasingly framed as Catholic Spain versus Protestant England. And it was close enough to England's own fragile colonial ambitions—Roanoke, struggling to exist—to feel like a threat. Drake didn't need St. Augustine to be rich. He needed it to be gone, or at least afraid.

So the town became a pawn in a larger war—one fought not only with armies in Europe but also with fire along the American shore. When Drake's fleet appeared in June 1586, it carried the weight of an empire's clash. St. Augustine was simply where that clash reached land.

After Drake's attack, Spain retreated strategically up the coast. Within a year, Spain abandoned its only remaining settlement, Santa Elena (near today's Parris Island), and relocated its remaining settlers to St. Augustine. It was an effort to consolidate what it could still defend. In practical terms, this was the turning point: Spain's Atlantic coastline experiment contracted back to its southern anchor, and the larger dream of a string of Spanish towns along the eastern seaboard lost momentum.

But St. Augustine was not finished. After Drake's fires burned it to embers, the town did what frontier towns always do—it began again. Timber was cut, and roofs were raised. The plaza filled once more with barter and rumor, and children returned from the woods. Corn was measured out. The ash layer settled into the soil and became part of the ground.

Archaeology confirms Drake's ruin in a way no chronicle can soften: beneath later streets and later houses, excavators in 2024 found burned floors capped by a thick charcoal/ash layer, with scorched Spanish and Indigenous ceramics and other fire-damaged material—an unmistakable signature of the 1586 destruction.[4]

Then nature took its turn. Hurricanes rolled in from the Atlantic with the indifference that had always ruled this coast. Storm surge swallowed docks, lifted roofs, and drowned crops. Disease followed the flood. Drought followed the wind. St. Augustine fell into a rhythm that would define it for generations: destruction, rebuilding, destruction, rebuilding. The town was never finished. It was always recovering.

Still, Spain knew that while it could survive hurricanes and pirates, it might not survive England. So Philip II of Spain made one last, sweeping gamble. In 1588, he launched the Armada—a fleet of unprecedented scale intended to crush Protestant England, restore Catholic dominance, and end the privateering war at its source. If England fell, men like Drake would be silenced. Spanish Florida would no longer be exposed on a contested Atlantic edge. The empire's perimeter would harden.

The Armada sailed north under banners heavy with confidence. It did not return that way.

Storms scattered it, and English ships harried it. The great fleet limped home, shattered. The message crossed the ocean: Spain was powerful, but not invincible. England was not a nuisance—it was a rival. St. Augustine understood what that meant.

The defeat of the Armada did not immediately undo Spain's empire. Silver still crossed the Atlantic, Havana still guarded the treasure fleets, and St. Augustine still flew the royal banner. Yet something had shifted.

Illustration, Spanish Armada

After 1588, England was no longer a reckless upstart. It was a durable enemy, with ships, capital, and colonies. The Atlantic was no longer Spain's corridor alone; it had become a contested highway. And St. Augustine—small, stubborn, perpetually rebuilding—sat directly on that highway.

So Spain did what empires do when they sense vulnerability: it fortified. In the coming decades, St. Augustine evolved from wooden palisades to heavier defenses. Timber forts rotted and were rebuilt. Hurricanes knocked them down; carpenters raised them again. The mission system expanded inland, binding the Timucua provinces more tightly to the capital. Corn flowed south along dusty roads, and Indigenous labor carried stone, timber, and supplies. The town endured through constant negotiation—between governor and friar, between Spanish official and Native cacique, between survival and ambition.

In the late 1590s, the town stood on the brink again—the population was thin, supplies uncertain, and the line between "colony" and "failure" remained narrow enough to step across.

New Native groups, including the Guale from the north and the Timucua from nearby mission provinces, were brought to St. Augustine in an effort to reshape the land. Marsh and swampland were cleared, drained, and coaxed into fields. Maize grew where standing water once collected. Labor and agricultural knowledge—Indigenous, not Spanish—transformed the settlement from a garrison dependent on shipments into a community that could feed itself. For a while, St. Augustine settled into a cautious but optimistic existence.

Gaule Uprising, 1597

In 1597, a newly appointed governor, Gonzalo Méndez de Canço, arrived in St. Augustine, determined to strengthen Indigenous alliances. He distributed gifts to native leaders to stabilize relations and expand mission influence. For a moment, it seemed the gospel model was working.

But in Guale territory along the Georgia coast, resentment had been simmering. Franciscan friars had begun challenging traditional marriage customs, particularly the practice of taking multiple wives among elite men. When one Guale leader was ordered to dismiss a second wife, the humiliation was public and political. Authority was not merely religious; it was social. Four months after the governor's arrival, the Guale uprising of 1597 erupted. Missionaries were killed, churches burned, and Spanish authority shaken.

The rebellion revealed the limits of spiritual empire. Gifts could build alliances, and doctrine could sanctify rule. But cultural transformation imposed too quickly could ignite resistance. St. Augustine survived by leaning—again—on Native power. What saved it was not gold. It was corn.

Doña María Meléndez, Timicua Cacica

The governor then turned to Timucua leadership for provisions.

Doña María Meléndez was a Timucua noblewoman and cacica—chieftainess—of the town of Nombre de Dios. By 1606, she appears as a ruler with influence along the coast between St. Augustine and roughly Cumberland Island. She was Christian, and her mother, who ruled before her, was among the earliest Timucua converts. Doña María had even married a Spanish soldier, revealing how Spanish influence could reshape Indigenous politics. This is the mission world at its most complicated: conversion and alliance, marriage and governance, Native authority recast through Spanish needs.

Artist rendering of Doña Maria

Through her intervention, something remarkable happened. One year before Jamestown, St. Augustine exported corn. Maize left St. Augustine bound for other Spanish outposts—an Atlantic trade in food rather than silver. While Jamestown starved in its early seasons, St. Augustine was shipping food. It was no longer merely clinging to life; it was contributing. That is continuity as power.

With stability came more institutions. A parish school taught children—Spanish, Native, mixed-heritage—catechism and literacy. A small, imperfect hospital opened, but it was real. These are not the markers of conquest but of permanence.

By mid-century, St. Augustine stood alone on Florida's Atlantic coast. But the seventeenth century would not be gentle.

1656, Timucua Rebellion

Disease continued to thin Native populations, and English-allied Indigenous raiders probed Spanish mission territory. Slaving raids tore through fragile Native communities. The Timucua towns and missions that had stretched inland and once protected St. Augustine began to collapse under pressure.

For the Timucua and Apalachee, it was the turning point. From populous, regionally powerful societies to communities battered by epidemic mortality, labor demands, and war. Forced into new geographies and new identities. For coastal and Gulf peoples farther south—the Tocobaga, Calusa, Tequesta, Ais—the story is different in detail but similar in trajectory: Spanish contact disrupted trade and diplomacy, introduced disease, and pulled Florida into a continental struggle in which people became strategic assets or targets. The mission system that had once promised protection became a target—and for many groups, a trap.

For decades, the mission world north and west of St. Augustine had been sold as a spiritual project of church bells, catechisms, and order. On the ground, it was also a labor system: people moved into mission towns, fields were expected to produce surplus, and men were compelled to haul goods, build, and serve.

Chiefs watched their authority erode as Spanish soldiers and officials treated their provinces as granaries and a workforce for the colonial capital. By mid-century, the Timucua world was stretched to the breaking point.

Then came the spark: a new round of demands— provisions, transport, and obedience—issued in the usual imperial tone, as if the people on the other end were still numerous, healthy, and obliged to comply. The frontier finally snapped.

The principal Timucua leader, Lucas Menéndez, said it plainly: he complained he was "no longer cacique [chief] of Timucua," and that "no attention" was paid to him.[5] That is not wounded pride. In Timucua political life, attention was power. It meant tribute, counsel, and recognition. When the

Spanish governor could ignore a paramount chief, it meant the old leverage had collapsed.

Additionally, Diego de Rebolledo, the governor of St. Augustine, was widely despised. Timucua leaders spoke of him with bitterness. He governed as if trying to squeeze water from a stone. When he demanded the immediate activation of the standing Indian militia, ordering each warrior to personally transport his own corn, Lucas Menéndez heard more than wartime mobilization. He heard a chain tightening.

Illustration, Timuca People

Lucas began working the old political web of messengers moving town to town, conversations among chiefs, and a shared argument: the governor intended to enslave them. Whether that was Rebolledo's literal goal almost didn't matter. In a world where mission labor already felt coercive, where disease had gutted families, and where Spanish officials treated Native leaders like foremen, "enslavement" was the logical endpoint.

What's striking is that the Timucua's first move wasn't violence. It was a diplomatic refusal—formal, deliberate, and political. A letter was drafted and sent to the governor by two messengers. A Franciscan friar—apparently sympathetic or alarmed by where this was heading—sent a supporting letter of his own alongside it. The crisis had grown so severe that even within the mission system, the moral and practical costs were impossible to ignore.

To Rebolledo, however, diplomacy wasn't an option. If one province refused, others might follow. The refusal wasn't treated as negotiation but as insubordination. He didn't bargain; he doubled down. The order was reissued, punishment was threatened, and he made clear that his authority would be enforced, not discussed.

The rebellion that followed was the moment of a collapsing political bargain—first in words, then, when words were dismissed, in blood.

The uprising did not erupt in a single village. Spanish testimony indicates it spread through multiple Timucua mission towns west of St. Augustine, particularly in the provinces of Timucua and Yustaga, along the inland corridor linking the capital to Apalachee. Messages were carried from town to town. Leaders coordinated timing, signaling not a spontaneous riot but an organized attempt to break the system binding them to the presidio. The targets were deliberate. Friars—visible agents of Spanish authority—were killed. Mission churches, the architectural heart of the colonial order, were attacked. Tribute stores and symbols of ecclesiastical control were destroyed.

The rebellion did not "win," but it changed everything. For a brief period, the inland communications network faltered, and travel between St. Augustine and the western provinces became uncertain. Spanish correspondence reflects alarm that the chain of Christianized towns—so carefully constructed over decades—might unravel. If the Timucua towns withdrew their compliance, the presidio would lose food, manpower, and its defensive buffer against rival European powers. The revolt was contained, but in that moment it exposed the vulnerability of Spanish Florida: a colony dependent not on overwhelming force but on fragile alliances sustained by negotiation, coercion, and faith.

Spanish authorities responded with investigations, arrests, executions, and forced reorganization. The mission network—already fragile—was restructured to serve St. Augustine's security and logistics more directly. Communities were relocated closer to the Camino Real, the road linking the interior to the capital, transforming once-autonomous towns into monitored way-stations that fed and serviced the colonial system. In other words, after 1656, the missions became less a frontier of conversion and more a corridor of control.

For St. Augustine, the city had relied on the mission provinces as a buffer, receiving food, labor, and intelligence between the capital and enemies approaching from the north. The buffer weakened at the worst possible time. A reduced, relocated, and destabilized Timucua landscape left St. Augustine more exposed, less provisioned, and less warned, just as English-allied raiding pressures were intensifying.

For the Timucua, it meant adaptation. They did not disappear into submission but remained a pivotal external force—trading partners one season, adversaries the next. Spanish demands for food, labor, and conversion continued to test the limits of tolerance. Indigenous leaders recalculated constantly: when to accommodate, when to resist, and when to strike hard enough to remind the newcomers whose land this still was.

St. Augustine lived in this tension, a settlement learning, season by season, how to survive within a Native political world that had not surrendered. The city that had nearly burned in its infancy endured not because it was welcomed, but because it, too, adapted to the reality that it stood inside someone else's world.

May 29, 1668, Matanzas Bay

At dawn on a summer morning, the English privateer Robert Searle slipped into Matanzas Bay and struck a town that had grown complacent behind its wooden defenses. St. Augustine's fortifications were still largely timber and earth. Searle's force moved quickly. They seized the settlement, looted homes and storehouses, stripped the church of valuables, and carried off prisoners for ransom. Buildings burned. Residents were killed. The attack lasted only days, yet it exposed how vulnerable the town truly was.

The raid was not random piracy; it was geopolitical pressure made visible. England had established itself in Charles Town in 1670, but even before that formal foothold, English privateers had already operated aggressively along Spain's claimed coastline. Searle's attack confirmed a hard truth: St. Augustine could not rely on distance or imperial prestige for protection.

It was now the only Spanish settlement remaining on the Atlantic coast. Spain's northern Atlantic ventures—most notably Santa Elena in present-day South Carolina—had already failed and been abandoned in the 1580s. There were no sister settlements between Florida and the Chesapeake. The Spanish frontier had contracted southward. St. Augustine stood alone. There would be no reinforcements from sister colonies up the coast.

The psychological shock was as significant as the physical damage. Spanish officials immediately recognized that wooden walls and small garrisons were insufficient. Calls for stronger defenses intensified. Within a few years, construction began on the masonry fortress that still defines the city—the Castillo de San Marcos, built of coquina stone to withstand cannon fire and coastal assault.

Searle's raid did not destroy St. Augustine. It forced Spain
to decide whether to abandon the settlement as it had
others or to fortify it permanently. Spain chose stone.

St. Augustine had to become a fortress. Under Philip IV
and later Charles II of Spain, funds were finally directed
toward something permanent. In 1672, construction began
on Castillo de San Marcos, a massive fortress rising beside
Matanzas Bay. Built of coquina stone quarried from
Anastasia Island, the fortress was raised by Spanish
soldiers, Indigenous workers, and Africans, both free and
enslaved, with walls thick enough to absorb cannon fire
rather than splinter. For twenty-three years, the fort grew,
bastion by bastion, until its completion.

The tallest watchtower at the fort is at the corner facing the outlet to the
Atlantic Ocean. National Park Service, Public Domain.

By the time the English colony of Carolina appeared on the
Atlantic map, the English invasion was already old news.
Plymouth had proved that England could plant a colony
and keep feeding it with more ships and more people. The
small settlement had gone from 300 to 20,000 people within
a generation. After that came the demographic engine
Spain could not match—England's Atlantic pipeline.

And yet one structure never truly fell silent. From 1572
until 1702, the parish church operated without
interruption. Storms came and went. Raids flared, and
governors rotated through. But Mass was celebrated,
baptisms were recorded, and marriages solemnized. Bells
rang. The church was not merely a building—it was the one
institution that insisted the town was permanent even
when its walls were not.

[1] National Parks Service
[2] Florida Museum of Natural History, University of Florida.
[3] Johnson, Betty Drees (1961). A Survey of Sir Francis Drake's Raid on St. Augustine, Florida, 1586. University of Stetson.
[4] WUWF Public Media, "The British Arrive at St. Augustine," Unearthing Florida, April 4, 2024.
[5] Manucy, Albert, Menendez, (1983), St. Augustine Historical Society.

4

English Expansion: 1675-1700

Land is the only thing in the world that amounts to anything, for it's the only thing in this world that lasts. It's the only thing worth working for, worth fighting for.

— Margaret Mitchell

ENGLAND WAS JUST GETTING started. Beginning in the 1640s, English migration and settlement accelerated. Virginia expanded up the Chesapeake, New England towns multiplied, and Barbados exploded as a sugar colony. By the 1650s, English America wasn't a string of experiments anymore. It was a growing belt of ports, farms, and militias that could push outward—into Native homelands and, eventually, toward Spanish Florida.

Spain saw it. The question is why Spain didn't stop it.

It is tempting to pin the change on a single king. But Florida's slow slide down Spain's priority list was not the decision of one distracted monarch. It was the cumulative drift of an overextended empire spanning three reigns.

When Philip III inherited the throne in 1598, Florida had already been designated as a defensive expense. It did not produce silver or sugar. It generated no revenue at all. It existed to guard the Bahama Channel and to signal Spain's claim along the Atlantic coast. In Madrid's ledgers, St. Augustine was not an asset but a line item.

Under Philip IV (1621–1665), the empire's bandwidth narrowed further. For much of the seventeenth century, Spain's attention was fixed not on Florida's sandy coast but on Europe—where the real stakes, as Madrid understood them, were measured in dynasties and armies. The Spanish Netherlands trembled under pressure. Italy demanded garrisons. Protestant and Catholic powers maneuvered for advantage in a balance that could tip the continent into open war. Money and men flowed east across the Atlantic not because Florida was unimportant but because Europe was existential. And wars are expensive.

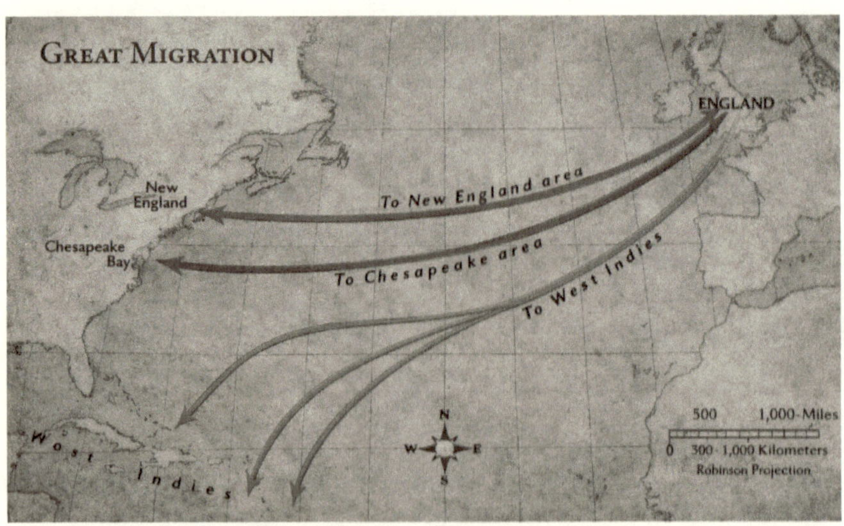

Map of European Great Migration 1640s

Then there were the mainland empires themselves—
New Spain and Peru. That was where revenue flowed. That
was where cities stood in stone, cathedrals rose,
universities functioned, and bureaucracies operated with
scale. Rebellion in Mexico or Peru would shake the empire
at its core. An English foothold in Virginia, by contrast,
looked peripheral—irritating, yes, but not fatal. Florida sat
in the middle of this hierarchy. Important but not lucrative.
Strategic but not productive. A shield, not a source of
wealth.

When English settlers multiplied along the upper
Atlantic coast—when Plymouth survived, when New
England towns proliferated, when English migration
surged in the mid-1600s—Spain noticed. But to intervene
decisively would require ships, soldiers, and sustained
commitment. Those assets were already committed
elsewhere. Madrid made a calculation.

Better to hold Havana firmly and guard the silver fleets.
Better to secure Mexico and Peru. Spain's silver was
extracted from mines in Mexico and Peru and shipped
across the ocean in convoys guarded like sacred relics.
Those fleets were the empire's bloodstream. Lose them,
and Spain bled out. So Havana mattered more than St.
Augustine. The Bahama Channel mattered more than a
mission province inland. Resources were funneled toward
the treasure route: ships, fortifications, and naval patrols.
Florida was funded just enough to protect that corridor, not

enough to expand. St. Augustine would endure as a forward watchtower rather than an expanding frontier.

Strategic gravity pulled Spain south and west.

Spain also became entangled in European wars that threatened its position in the Spanish Netherlands and Italy. Armies had to be paid, fleets maintained, and diplomacy financed. Silver from Mexico and Peru was stretched thin. Governors in St. Augustine wrote petitions for reinforcements and repairs; replies from Madrid were slow, partial, or apologetic.

The pattern was clear: defend Havana, defend the treasure fleets, defend Mexico and Peru. Florida would receive what was left.

Then came Charles II of Spain (1665–1700), who inherited an empire weakened by decades of strain. By the time he took the throne, Spain's administrative machine was brittle, its finances exhausted, and its military stretched thin. If Florida had struggled for attention before, it struggled even more now—not because Charles II singled it out for neglect, but because there was less capacity to go around.

Meanwhile, across the Atlantic, England was consolidating. New England had multiplied. The "Great Migration" had filled the northern coast with towns, farms, and militia companies. Under Charles II of England, expansion turned decisively southward. In 1663, he granted the Carolina charter, and in 1670, settlers founded Charleston. That single settlement altered the southern

frontier. It planted an English base much closer to Spanish
Florida and, crucially, to the mission provinces that fed St.
Augustine. English traders, settlers, and allied Native
groups now stood much closer to Spanish mission
territory.

From that point forward, pressure didn't come only by
sea. It came overland—through trade, alliances, and
eventually slaving raids that tore through the Indigenous
buffer Spain relied on. St. Augustine faced a new reality:
English America wasn't passing through. It was settling in.

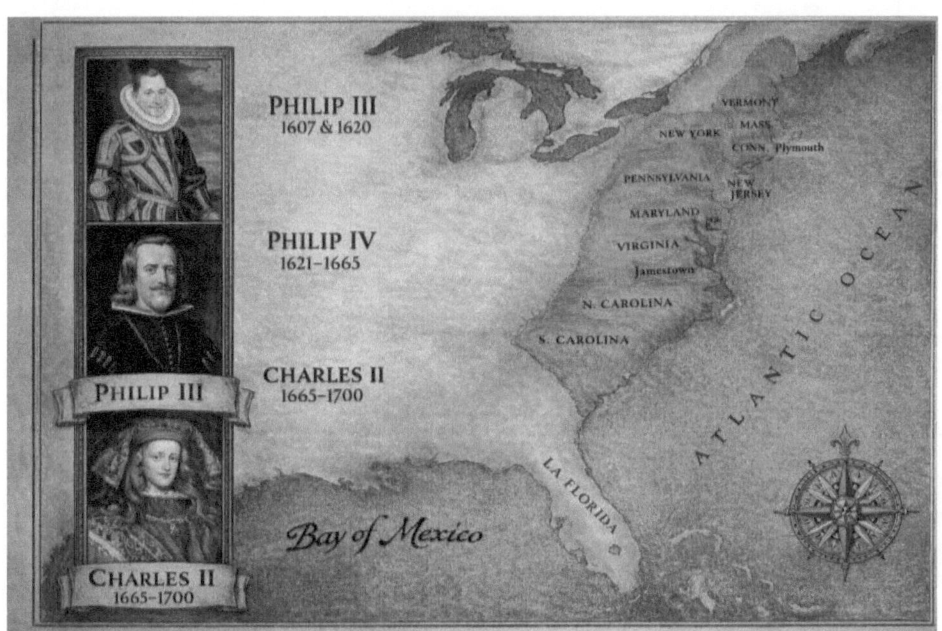

Timeline of Atlantic Coast Expansion and Spanish Rulers

So the shift was not a single king abandoning its claim to
North America. Spain's gaze remained fixed on Europe and
the silver fleets. Meanwhile, England invested where it

could expand. By the late seventeenth century, the upper Atlantic coast was solidly English—not because Spain failed to see the threat, but because it lacked the will and resources to uproot it.

St. Augustine felt that shift as tightening pressure. The mission provinces thinned under English-backed raids. Trade routes destabilized, and the buffer north of the city eroded.

❖

Black Militia, 1683

In 1683, St. Augustine counted its defenders. The town had been burned before. English raiders had come down from Carolina with fire and impatience, testing Spain's hold on Florida and finding it thin. The garrison was small, and the population smaller. Indigenous alliances shifted with the seasons, making the frontier violent and close. Spain needed bodies capable of bearing arms and watchers on the marshes. It needed proof—to Havana, Madrid, and Charleston—that Florida was not undefended.

By this time, St. Augustine's Black population included men born in Iberia and Africa, men who had escaped from English plantations, men who were free, and men whose status was not entirely settled. The categories did not disappear in Florida; they blurred. They were quarrying stone, hauling timber, farming provision plots, and serving in households. They were visible, necessary, and increasingly experienced in navigating borderland violence.

Illustration, Black Militia Man

In the 1680s, St. Augustine was a garrison town, thinly manned, often hungry, and always looking over its shoulder at English expansion. It existed only to guard sea lanes and frustrate Protestant rivals. It needed labor and loyalty. So the governor did something practical. He mustered a militia. And it was made up entirely of free Black men.

The record is spare, but muster rolls, references in correspondence, and administrative notation confirm its existence: an all-Black militia, organized in a Spanish colony decades before the English mainland would contemplate arming enslaved men for its own defense.[1]

A musket and a uniform marked a shift in status: to stand in formation under the king's banner was to move from one category to another—from labor asset to military subject. A man who stood guard on the town's perimeter and was listed on a muster roll as a militiaman occupied a different place in the social order than one listed as property.

Wages, rations, and drills stitched Black residents into the colony's defensive structure. The arrangement was not abolition, and it did not dissolve slavery in Spanish Florida. It was transactional. Service for security and loyalty for recognition. But it altered the arithmetic.

They were trained to drill, to fire, to patrol the approaches to town. The existence of the Black militia also sent a message north. Runaways who reached Florida might not simply disappear into kitchens or quarries. They might be armed and uniformed. They might return fire.

St. Augustine's all-Black militia was born not of idealism but of necessity. By the early eighteenth century, this policy culminated in the founding of Fort Mose—the first legally sanctioned free Black settlement in what would become the United States. But before Fort Mose, before free Black militias stood under the Spanish flag, another, more troubling undercurrent ran along the Atlantic corridor.

❖

The Southern Railroad

Long before the Underground Railroad in the North, there was another underground route running south.

Shaped by Catholic doctrine and imperial strategy, Spanish Florida offered sanctuary to enslaved people who converted to Catholicism and agreed to serve the Spanish Crown. In practice, this recognized the possibility of freedom, even if it did not abolish slavery itself. Black men and women in Florida also experienced a legal regime very different from the one hardening in English Carolina and Virginia. Spanish legal culture allowed manumission, interracial marriage, and limited mobility among enslaved Africans.

This was the crucial difference between Spain and England. As slave labor systems across the English Southeast expanded and hardened, slave codes stiffened, and racial categories calcified into law. Punishments were no longer improvisations; they became policy. The British system was becoming hereditary and total, defining Blackness itself as enslavement.

Florida stood in uneasy contrast: still a slaveholding society, still dependent on coerced labor, but also a place where free Black households multiplied, where Black militia units drilled in defense of the town, where wages were sometimes earned and contracts recorded. The differences born of competing imperial visions.

The colonies tightened their grip and increased patrols. The message was unmistakable: there was nowhere to run. But news travels. Along Indigenous trading paths, in the holds of small boats, in the whispered conversations of dockworkers and field hands, the rumor moved southward: in Florida, the Spanish did not always send runaways back. In Florida, you had a chance.

October, 1687

The first boat came in by water at night. A small vessel sliding toward the inlet, sitting low in the water with too many bodies aboard. Eight men, two women, and a nursing child. They had slipped out of Carolina and aimed south, trusting rumor and God.

The English later wrote down their names—Conano, Jesse, Jacque, Gran Domingo, Cambo, Mingo, Dicque, Robi. Governor Diego de Quiroga did not return them immediately. He questioned them and examined their intentions. The men were assigned to the quarry, where they hauled and shaped coquina under a hard sun. Two were placed with a blacksmith—suggesting skill, not just muscle. The women were put into domestic service in Spanish households. And then the crucial detail: they were paid. Not richly. Not as equals. But paid.[2]

Their status hung in the balance. English law called them slaves. Spanish officials began treating them as something else—subjects in the making, conditional allies. Employment became evidence.

Illustration, Free Black Resident of Saint Augustine

When an English agent arrived demanding their return, Quiroga refused. He argued that they had converted, formed families, and were "usefully employed." The phrase is clinical and bureaucratic, yet it carries force. Usefulness was protection. In that refusal, the border shifted.

This was not yet a formal royal decree. That would come later. In 1687, it was still improvisation—governor against governor, empire against empire, bodies at the center of the argument. The fugitives had not reached a utopia. They had reached a calculation.

But it was enough. They had crossed from certainty into possibility. More fugitives would keep arriving, slipping through swamps that English patrols could not fully control. As they appeared in greater numbers, Spanish officials saw more than desperate men and women slipping out of the Carolina swamps. Now they saw leverage.

Each arrival weakened the English economy. Each converted fugitive strengthened Spain's claim to moral authority in the Catholic–Protestant contest. Each able-bodied man added muscle to the quarry and the ramparts of the Castillo, and each woman placed in a household became part of the town's fabric. The frontier made everyone a pragmatist.

The paperwork followed. English agents demanded return of "their property," sending their pleas to Madrid. Spanish replies leaned on religion and sovereignty: if these people embraced Catholicism and pledged loyalty to the king, they were now Spain's subjects. Not cargo.

On November 7, 1693, Charles II formally granted liberty to runaways (men and women) in Florida, finalizing what the governors had been improvising on the ground.[3] Runaways who accepted baptism and agreed to serve the Spanish crown could receive freedom. It was conditional, required obedience, and military readiness. It was empire speaking, not abolition. But in the rice fields of Carolina, that distinction didn't matter.

So they came—not because Florida was gentle, but because it offered a different calculus. A narrow door instead of a locked gate. It offered a place where wages might be paid, and conversion could become a shield. Labor on a stone fortress could transform status from hunted to protected.

Florida, 1690

But there's another uneasy story to tell. Spain, like England, participated in the transatlantic slave trade.

Some arrived through Spanish Atlantic networks, while others came indirectly from the Caribbean by way of Havana and Santo Domingo. They entered through the imperial circuits of licensed traders, private merchants, and military supply ships. They were skilled carpenters, field hands, cooks, or interpreters.

Some had first touched Spanish soil in the Caribbean before being carried north to the thin, sandy edge of the empire called Florida. By the turn of the eighteenth century, the question was no longer whether slavery would shape the region—it already had—but whose version of slavery, and whose version of freedom, would prevail.

While English colonies would enshrine racial slavery into law and economy, Spanish Florida left legal space for freedom, conversion, and upward mobility within a Catholic framework. It was imperfect, hierarchical, and imperial—but it was not identical to the chattel and plantation regimes forming to the north. St. Augustine became a laboratory of empire, law, race, and resistance.

The Legacy

For more than a century, from 1565 through the closing years of the seventeenth century, Florida's early history defies clean categories.

From de Soto's early brutality to eventual mission diplomacy, and from Native uprisings to African sanctuary, Spain enslaved. But it also converted. Spain punished, but it sheltered. African men and women endured bondage—and, in other cases, carved out freedom decades before the American Revolution.

Africans were woven into the fabric of St. Augustine from the beginning—not as a single class or condition, but across a spectrum. Whether free, enslaved, or somewhere in between, they served as godparents in parish books and married beneath the church's vaulted ceiling. They baptized children and built families. They worked as tradesmen and earned wages—sometimes. They even bore arms in the militia.

Illustration of a mixed race Family, Saint Augustine

Women appear in the record, too—placed in households, standing as sponsors, crossing swamps with nursing infants, and forging kin networks that held the town together in quieter ways. The archive is thin, but the pattern is not. Over a hundred years, Africans in St.

Augustine forged lives that encompassed labor and love, faith and defense, constraint and opportunity.

By 1700, St. Augustine stood as something unusual on the North American coast: a Spanish, Catholic, multiethnic garrison town where Native, African, and European lives were entangled by law, faith, and survival. It had been improvised, uneven, and conditional. It was never a segregated society; its inhabitants were bound together by necessity and proximity. It was Catholic and Atlantic, yes, but also local, shaped daily by Native knowledge and Native kinship. America's true beginning was integrated, fragile, and interwoven from the start.

The century ahead, however, would bring sharper lines. The Atlantic was sending something larger toward the peninsula: a system of human labor built on scale. When that system arrived in force, it would test everything St. Augustine thought it knew about freedom.

———————————◆———————————

At the close of the century, St. Augustine was no longer simply surviving. It was a fortress holding a line—between Protestant and Catholic, between English and Spanish, between survival and erasure. The long shift had happened quietly—over decades, across reigns, through budgets and wars fought an ocean away. It was a walled garrison city, a Catholic stronghold on a crowded coast. African soldiers stood guard alongside Spaniards. Native allies still moved through the plaza, though their numbers were smaller now and their world irrevocably altered. And St. Augustine, as always, stood where empires meet, and budgets run out.

But the contrast was stark: while Spain held St. Augustine and a mission corridor, England continued to extend English occupation along the upper Atlantic coast through sheer accumulation: more settlers, ships, farms, and greater political permanence. English America was rapidly expanding through migration, but Spanish Florida was merely holding its ground. By now the "upper coast" was effectively beyond Spanish reach.

The City That Would Not Fall

San Marcos de Castillo

Then, as the century closed, the pressure tightened once more. English Carolina had grown bold. Raids into Spanish mission territory intensified. The fragile northern provinces—the very lands that had once sustained the capital—were being dismantled. St. Augustine had survived Drake. It had survived hurricanes, rebellion, famine, and imperial overreach. It had hardened from timber to stone. But the Atlantic world was changing faster than walls could rise.

The next storm would not come from the sea alone.

[1] Cyndi Reigelsperger, Interethnic Relations and Settlement on the Spanish Florida Frontier (PhD diss., University of Florida, 2013).

[2] Jane Landers, Black Society in Spanish Florida (Urbana: University of Illinois Press, 1999)

[3] Jane Landers, "Spanish Sanctuary: Fugitives in Florida, 1687–1790," Florida Historical Quarterly 62, no. 3 (1984).

Part II— Tides of Empire

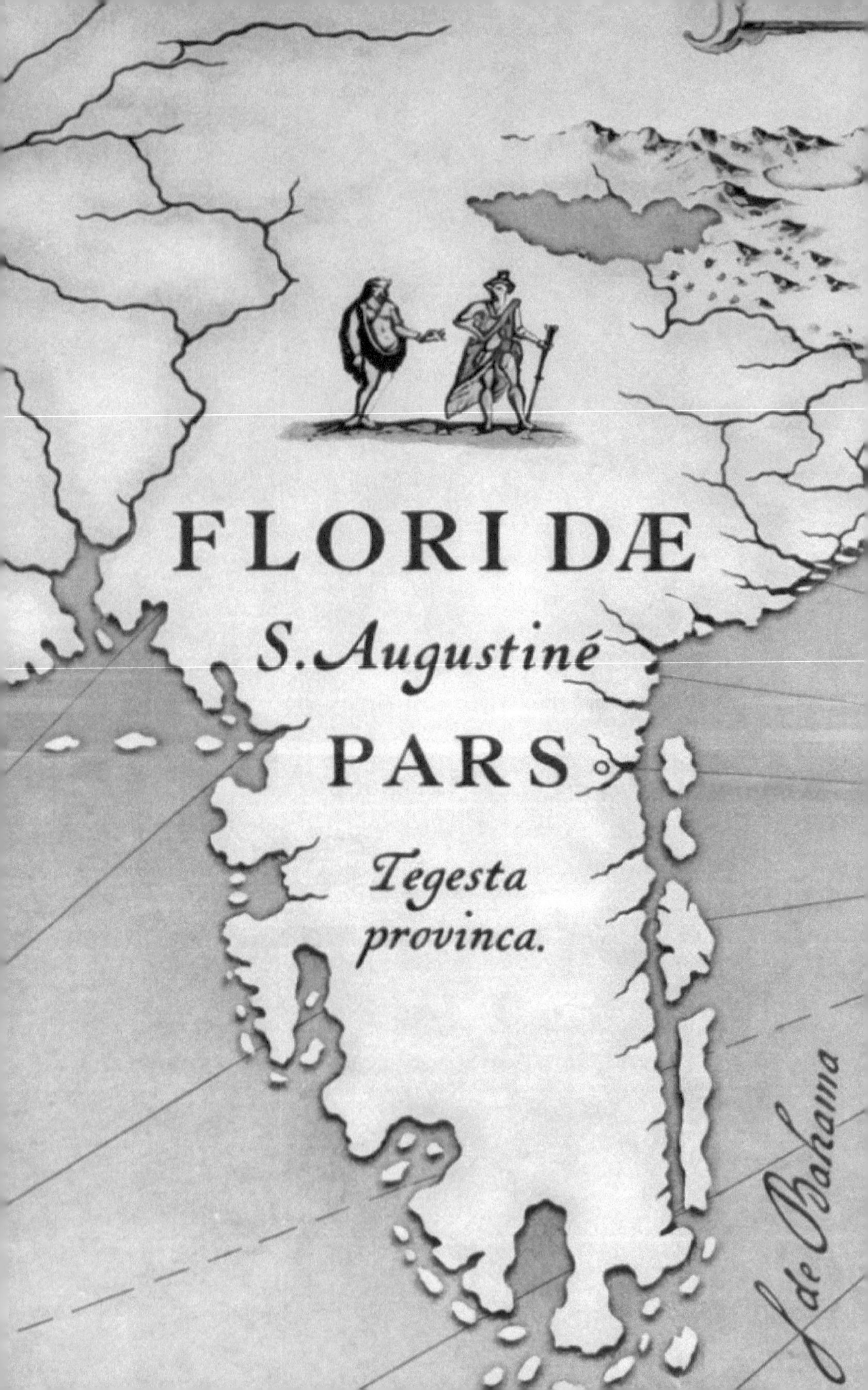

FLORIDÆ
S. Augustiné
PARS
Tegesta
provinca.
I. de Bahama

5

1700-1750: Endurance

Come what may, all bad fortune is to be conquered by endurance.

—Virgil

In the year 1700, ST. AUGUSTINE was no longer an experiment. It was an old town by American standards. Nearly 150 years after its founding, the children born under Spanish rule were now grandparents. The parish bells of San Agustín had rung through famine, pirate raids, English invasions, and epidemic disease. Across the Atlantic world, colonies rose and failed with dizzying speed. Yet here, on a narrow barrier island facing the Atlantic, Spain's outpost endured. Not wealthy. Not large. But enduring.

Contrast that with Jamestown and Plymouth Colony — the twin pillars of the English origin story. Jamestown nearly collapsed in its first years, undone by hunger, disease, and mismanagement. The winter of 1609–1610 entered memory as the "Starving Time," when desperate settlers ate rats, leather, and, according to archaeological evidence, even one another.[1] Plymouth fared little better at the outset; nearly half its settlers died in the first winter. Survival in both places depended on Indigenous alliances and imported labor systems that would soon harden into plantation slavery.

Illustration, Saint Augustine, Colonial era

The mythology would come later. Jamestown became the cradle of representative government; Plymouth, the seed of religious liberty. Thanksgiving replaced famine. The Virginia House of Burgesses overshadowed the years of corporate misrule and extractive ambition that nearly destroyed the colony. Its survival depended on tobacco profits, expanding land seizures, the forced labor of Africans, and the dispossession of Native peoples. The English colonies survived not because they were morally clearer or politically superior, but because they adapted quickly to systems that generated export wealth and demographic growth.

St. Augustine followed a different logic. It was never meant to be a profit engine. Spain planted it to guard sea lanes and convert souls, not to cultivate cash crops. Florida's sandy soil would never rival Virginia's tobacco fields or Carolina's rice plantations. The town survived because it was strategic, sitting like a sentry at the mouth of the Bahama Channel, watching over treasure fleets bound for Europe. When English privateers burned it, Spain rebuilt it. When wood proved too vulnerable, they quarried coquina and raised the Castillo de San Marcos—stone absorbing cannon fire that would have splintered English forts.

Its economy reflected that reality. St. Augustine depended on royal subsidies, the "situado," from Mexico. Soldiers' pay, food rations, and building materials: much of it came by ship from Havana or Veracruz. This dependence has often been read as a weakness, but in truth, it was a stabilizer. The town did not rise or fall on speculative crops or market booms. It survived on imperial obligation. While English colonists gambled on profit, Spaniards in Florida relied on policy and persistence. Survival, not expansion, was the goal.

Between 1700 and 1750, the English colonies along the Atlantic seaboard grew in population and wealth. They spread outward and inland. Florida, however, remained narrow and coastal, a defensive arc rather than an expanding frontier.

There were human costs embedded in both systems. English colonies expanded through land hunger, pushing westward and codifying racial slavery into law. Spanish Florida enslaved people as well, but operated under a different legal tradition. By the early 1700s, free Black families lived within and north of St. Augustine, serving in militia units that defended the town. The English borderlands hardened around racial hierarchy; the Spanish frontier remained more porous, if no less imperial.

War tested these differences. English Carolina launched repeated invasions in the early eighteenth century.

Meanwhile, Jamestown itself had faded. By the eighteenth century, it was no longer Virginia's political heart. Williamsburg had replaced it, and Plymouth, too, had been absorbed into the larger colony of Massachusetts Bay. The English origin points endured in memory more than in physical prominence. St. Augustine, by contrast, remained where it had always been—small, militarized, and watchful, yet still firmly planted where it had always been. It had outlasted failed French ventures, pirate strongholds, and English assaults. It had absorbed Africans, Spaniards, Indigenous converts, and refugees into a complex frontier society. It had endured not by accident, but by design.

---◆---

The Siege, 1702

The warning came from the woods, carried by a Choctaw woman who had been listening and watching the English. She had overheard the plan: an attack was coming.
In 1702, King Charles II of Spain died without an heir, sparking a war over the Spanish throne. By November, that imperial struggle spilled across the Atlantic and into the pine barrens of Florida.

South Carolina's governor, James Moore, saw Spain's distraction as an opportunity. It had already lost much of its Atlantic-claimed territory over a century of English expansion, and Florida stood in the way of Carolina's southern ambitions.

The town moved quickly. Nearly 1,500 residents of St. Augustine, including soldiers, friars, free Black militia, women, and children, fled into the Castillo de San Marcos. Outside, the English and their Native allies stormed through the countryside. The English had armed Native groups eager to settle scores and secure advantage, but the Spanish had long refused to distribute weapons widely among their mission communities.

The missions fell, and storehouses were looted. The imbalance was clear. By the time Moore's forces reached St. Augustine, much of the surrounding mission network lay in ruins.

Then the bombardment began. English artillery, more modern and better supplied, thundered against the fort's walls. Spanish guns answered, but many were outdated, their range and reliability inferior. The English burned the wooden houses clustered around the fortress, turning the town to smoke and embers.

Castillo de San Marcos

Yet the fort itself did not splinter. It was built of coquina—a shellstone quarried from nearby Anastasia Island—soft enough to absorb cannon fire rather than shatter under it. Where iron balls struck, they sank into the walls, leaving pocked impressions instead of breaches. The

English had expected cracks and collapse. Instead, they faced a fortress that swallowed impact after impact.

Inside, time stretched. Babies were born during the siege, one to a Native woman and a Black father, as life entered the world to the sound of artillery beyond the walls. The modest food supplies thinned, and water had to be rationed. The courtyard grew crowded with bodies and animals, and the air turned sour. Illness crept through the packed rooms.

A message was smuggled out by canoe under cover of night, slipping past English patrols, carrying a plea to Havana. If relief did not come, the town would starve behind its own defenses. It had been nearly 7 weeks since the siege began.

On a clear winter morning, it came on the horizon: four Spanish warships from Cuba, carrying troops, ammunition, and supplies. After fifty-two days, outgunned at sea and unable to breach the walls, the English withdrew. Before leaving, they set what remained of the town ablaze. When the gates of the Castillo opened, St. Augustine stepped back into ash. The fort was still standing. The city was not.

Recovery would take decades. Winter pressed in. Exposure, disease, and chronic ailments worsened in the damp aftermath. Fields had been destroyed; livestock had been scattered. The mission system that had once buffered the town was gone. But Moore was not finished. Humiliated by his failure to take the Castillo, he turned his aggression outward.

To finance the ongoing war against Spanish Florida, Governor James Moore increasingly relied on slave raiding.

In 1704, leading a mixed force of English colonists and Creek allies, he invaded the Apalachee mission province west of St. Augustine. The result was systematic destruction. Missions were burned. Several friars were killed. Apalachee towns were emptied. More than a thousand men, women, and children were captured and marched north into the expanding Carolina slave trade; many others fled, starved, or were absorbed into allied Native towns. Some Native groups, armed and entangled in shifting alliances, participated in capturing rivals. The violence was systematic and devastating.

The campaign shattered Spain's western Florida mission system. The Timucuan provinces, already weakened by disease and earlier warfare, collapsed soon after under continued pressure. By the end, much of interior Spanish Florida had been depopulated—not by accident or epidemic alone, but by deliberate slave raiding that tied Carolina's frontier economy to the capture and sale of humans.

Entire Indigenous landscapes across north Florida and southern Georgia had been emptied or broken. They had supplied corn to St. Augustine, but now the fields were barren. Food was scarce again.

Florida survived the siege, but the borderlands did not escape transformation. The 1702 attack was more than a failed assault on a fortress. It signaled the collapse of

Spain's mission frontier and the escalation of an English-backed slave economy that would reshape the Southeast. The coquina walls held against cannon fire, but they could not shield the wider world from the fire spreading beyond them.

❖

Fort Mose, 1738

Out of the smoke of siege and the violence along the frontier, Spain doubled down on a policy that unsettled the English more than cannon fire ever could.

In 1693, the Spanish Crown had formally promised freedom to enslaved people fleeing the English colonies if they accepted Catholicism and pledged service to Spain. By the 1730s, that promise required structure. Runaways were arriving in increasing numbers from Carolina and later Georgia—men and women who had risked swamps, patrols, and starvation to reach Spanish ground. They needed land, arms, and a defensible position. In 1738, Governor Manuel de Montiano authorized the creation of Fort Mose, two miles north of St. Augustine.[2] Its formal name was Gracia Real de Santa Teresa de Mose, and it carried both piety and politics.

A strategic fortification with a wooden palisade, it was positioned to serve as the northern defensive buffer for St. Augustine. Its residents were entirely free Black men and women, many formerly enslaved in English territories, organized into a militia company under Spanish command. They farmed small plots, raised families, and drilled with muskets. Freedom here was conditional—tied to loyalty, labor, and military service—but it was recognized in law. In a Southeast increasingly defined by hereditary racial slavery under English codes, Mose stood as a direct contradiction.

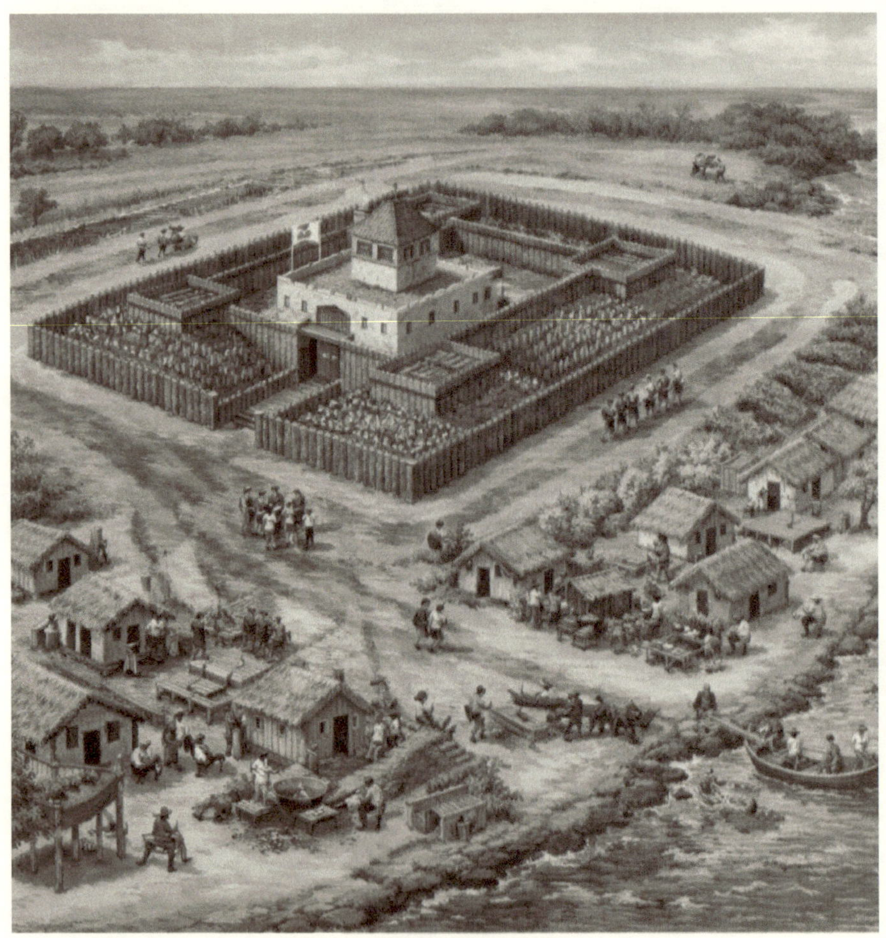

Illustration, Fort Mose

Francisco Menéndez

One of the men who would come to define Fort Mose's character was Francisco Menéndez. Born in West Africa around 1690, he was captured as a boy and transported into the English slave system in South Carolina. There, he learned English and Indigenous languages. He escaped once, slipping south into the contested borderlands and living among Native communities in the forests between Carolina and Florida. In that wilderness, he learned to track, hunt, and handle firearms with skill.

Illustration, Francisco Menéndez

He fought alongside Native allies during the Yamasee War, a violent 1715 uprising in which Native nations, angered by debt, land seizures, and the Indian slave trade, nearly destroyed the Carolina colony.

The Yamasee War reshaped the Southeast. English traders had armed Native groups and turned intertribal rivalries into a slave-raiding economy that funneled thousands of Indigenous captives into Atlantic markets. When that system collapsed into revolt, frontier alliances shifted overnight. Menéndez fought in that chaos, but when the war ended, and English power reasserted itself, he was captured and sold back into slavery.

He escaped, again, but this time, upon reaching Spanish Florida, he was purchased by a Spanish official who delayed or ignored his manumission. His knowledge of terrain and languages made him valuable property. He could read and write, understood English tactics and Native warfare, and in a colony constantly under threat from Carolina, those skills mattered.

When a new governor, Manuel de Montiano, took office in the 1730s, policy hardened in favor of sanctuary and structured defense. Black militiamen who had pledged loyalty to Spain were formally granted freedom. In 1738, Menéndez was manumitted and appointed captain of the Black militia at Fort Mose.[3] The title was not ceremonial. He commanded armed men on the northern edge of the Spanish frontier, responsible for guarding the road to St. Augustine.

Under his leadership, Fort Mose became more than a refuge. It became a disciplined community of farmers, soldiers, and families who had escaped plantation bondage and now defended the empire that sheltered them. Menéndez embodied the borderlands' contradictions: once enslaved by the English, briefly constrained even under Spanish authority, and finally free through military service.

But Spanish sanctuary policy did more than offer baptism and protection; it drained labor from the Carolina and Georgia plantations and undermined the racial order that sustained them. Each person who reached Florida was not only a refugee but also a loss—economic, political, and psychological. News of armed Black men serving the Spanish Crown spread quickly north. Planters feared not only escape but also the example.

Bloody Mose

In 1740, King George II of England wanted Spanish Florida neutralized. Georgia—young, ambitious, and strategically positioned—was to capture St. Augustine and end Spain's practice of freeing runaway slaves. General James Oglethorpe, founder of Georgia and a veteran of European wars, was given command. He moved south with British colonial troops, artillery, and Native allies. The objective was clear: take St. Augustine and break the precedent of Black freedom.

Fort Mose stood directly in the invasion's path. Its residents evacuated ahead of Oglethorpe's advance, retreating into St. Augustine. The British entered and occupied the empty fort without firing a single shot. For two weeks, it served as a forward position in Oglethorpe's broader siege strategy against the Castillo de San Marcos. From Mose, British forces could press the northern approaches and probe Spanish defenses. It briefly appeared that the English had achieved what South Carolina had failed to do decades earlier.

But the loss was temporary. Before dawn on June 26, Spanish regulars, allied Native fighters, and Black militiamen launched a coordinated pre-dawn assault on the British garrison occupying the ruined settlement.

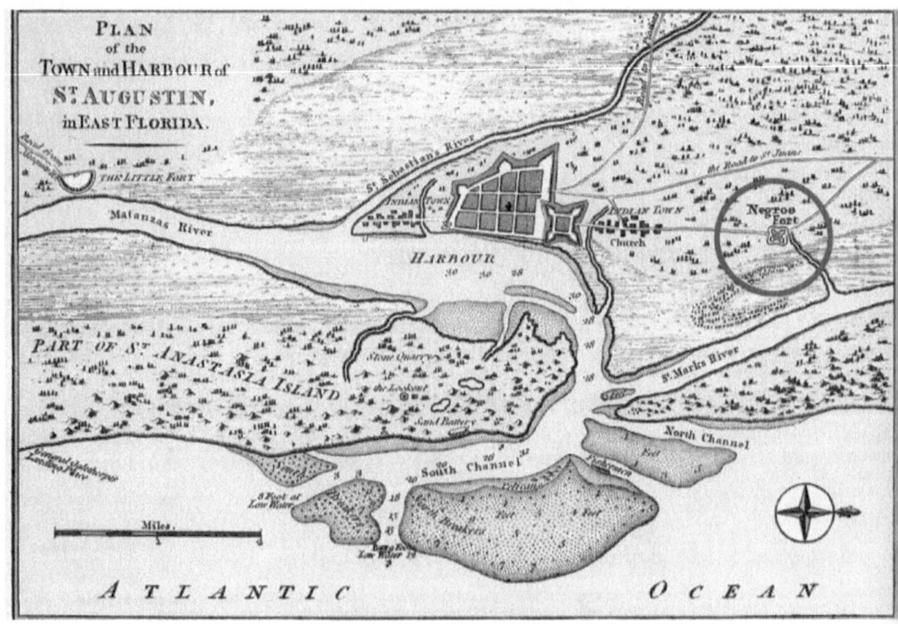

Illustration of St. Augustine and Fort Mose (circled)

Menéndez led the counterattack. In the darkness and close quarters, the fighting turned brutal. British troops were overwhelmed; Roughly seventy-five British soldiers and officers were killed in what became known as the Battle of Bloody Mose.

The counterstrike broke British momentum. Without firm control of Fort Mose and unable to breach the Castillo's coquina walls, the British siege unraveled. Within weeks, Oglethorpe withdrew north.

In time, the community of Fort Mose was rebuilt, its existence reaffirmed not only by Spanish law but by blood. Propaganda began almost immediately. English accounts emphasized ferocity, portraying the Black militiamen as savage, unrestrained, and excessive. The language was strategic. It reframed disciplined military resistance as barbarism and sought to undermine the legitimacy of Spain's sanctuary policy.

The irony was sharp: men who had fought under a Spanish commission in structured units were recast as lawless aggressors. The narrative would echo into the next century—violence attributed not to the instability of empire but to the supposed nature of the people resisting it.

Fort Mose itself did not survive intact. The settlement was damaged in the fighting and later abandoned; its residents were relocated within St. Augustine's defensive perimeter. The experiment in Black-led frontier defense had not failed, but it had been disrupted. Freedom on the border remained real yet precarious.

Menéndez's life mirrored that instability. Later in the ongoing frontier conflict, he was captured by English forces. Once identified as the leader at Mose, he was tortured—beaten, whipped, and reportedly subjected to salt and vinegar poured into open wounds. He was transported to the Bahamas and sold back into slavery. That might have ended the story. But Menéndez escaped again, made his way back to Spanish Florida, and resumed his military service. When Fort Mose was eventually reestablished, he returned as captain of its militia. His life became a cycle of captivity and reclamation, violence and command—a personal embodiment of the borderlands themselves.

By mid-century, the English had failed to crush St. Augustine or extinguish Spain's sanctuary policy. But the cost was evident. Fort Mose had been destroyed once and rebuilt. Its people had been displaced and then returned. The battle left more than bodies; it left competing narratives about who had the right to claim freedom.

The Marsh Speaks

Fort Mose is not only a story of flight and fortification but also one of recovery. For more than a century, its existence was more rumor than landscape, mentioned in Spanish records and remembered in fragments, yet physically swallowed by marsh and time. However, thanks to the work of modern archaeologists and scholars, it has come back into view.

In the mid-1980s, historian Jane Landers began the unglamorous work of sifting through archives, maps, and correspondence to pinpoint exactly where this "free Black town" had stood and who had lived there. Her archival finds, including census records listing residents, ages, and origins, shifted Mose from symbol to community, with actual people attached.[4]

Then the ground itself began to speak. Archaeologist Kathleen Deagan led major field investigations in the late 1980s that confirmed what paper alone can't prove: the fort's physical footprint, including its moat, earthen walls, and the traces of wooden buildings within. The archaeology does something narratives often skip: it shows daily life. Not just "a fort," but a place where people cooked, repaired tools, traded goods, and lived in structures that left patterns in soil and refuse.

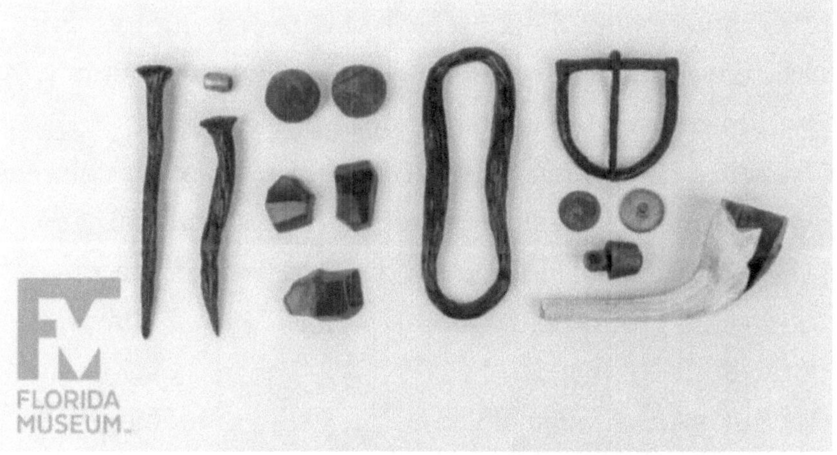

Artifacts recovered from Fort Mose, Florida Museum

Together, Landers and Deagan's work changed what the public saw—and what the public was forced to acknowledge. Fort Mose's rediscovery and documentation helped drive preservation and recognition. The site was designated a U.S. National Historic Landmark in 1994 and has since been recognized internationally through UNESCO's Slave Route "Site of Memory." Those designations matter not as trophies but as corrections — evidence that early American history did not run only through colonial New England and that Black freedom was organized, defended, and lived on Spanish soil decades before the Revolution.

Fort Mose did not erase slavery from Spanish Florida. Enslaved labor persisted in the colony, yet it reshaped the landscape of possibility. It showed that Black freedom — armed, organized, and legally sanctioned — could exist in North America 125 years before the Emancipation Proclamation. In the long contest between empires, Fort Mose was small in scale. In the history of freedom in what would become the United States, it was seismic.
By mid-century, tensions between Britain and its colonies would intensify, leading to revolution. When that war came, Florida would not stand apart. It would become contested ground once more — passed between empires, pulled into global conflict.

But as the English colonies prepared to redefine themselves, St. Augustine had already proven something older: that survival in America did not belong to any one language, church, or myth. The first enduring European city in what would become the United States was Spanish, stubborn, and still standing.

[1] Encyclopedia Virginia, "The Starving Time," Encyclopedia Virginia.

[2] Kathleen A. Deagan (2014). "Fort Mose: America's first Free Black Community". In Ann L.; Henderson Gary R. Mormino; Carlos J. Cano (eds.). Spanish Pathways in Florida, 1492-1992: Caminos Españoles en La Florida, 1492-1992. Pineapple Press.

[3] African Americans in St. Augustine 1565-1821". U.S. National Park Service. U.S. Department of the Interior.

[4] Jane Landers (1999). Black Society in Spanish Florida. University of Illinois Press.

6

1750-1800: Empires Collide

In every human breast, God has implanted a principle, which we call love of freedom.

— Phillis Wheatley

THE SEVEN YEARS' WAR didn't begin in Florida, but it ended Florida's first era. Fought from 1756 to 1763, it was a global struggle involving Europe, the Caribbean, North America, West Africa, and India. It was an imperial knife fight over trade routes, sugar islands, forts, and the right to tax and expand. In North America, Britain and France battled for the interior; in the Caribbean, they fought over ports that controlled fleets. Everywhere, the war exposed a simple truth of empire: far-off places were bargaining chips, and the people living in them rarely got a vote.

Spain entered late and paid the price immediately. In 1762, Britain struck where Spain could least afford to lose: Havana. The city was not just another colonial possession; it was the keystone of Spain's Caribbean defense and a critical port for Atlantic shipping. The British captured Havana and held it long enough to force a diplomatic reckoning. Spain was offered a hard trade: Britain would return Havana, but not for free. It would take Florida in return.

In 1763, under the terms of the Treaty of Paris, Spain ceded Florida to Britain in exchange for the return of Havana. In one stroke of the pen, Spain surrendered its long-held, costly Florida frontier.

That bargain illustrates how empires ranked their possessions. St. Augustine had endured for nearly two centuries, surviving raids, sieges, fires, famine, and the slow grind of frontier war. Yet on Spain's imperial balance sheet, it could never be Havana. Florida was strategic, yes, but it was also expensive and thinly provisioned, dependent on imperial subsidies and perpetually under pressure from British colonies to the north. Havana had wealth, ships, and leverage. Florida was defense—and a headache.

And so, in 1763, diplomacy finally achieved what English cannons could not. Britain acquired Florida on paper, and St. Augustine—Spain's oldest North American city—was transferred not by conquest but by treaty.[1] The war that redrew maps from Canada to India also redrew the future of Florida, setting the stage for the British period that would, in turn, collide with the unrest brewing in Britain's mainland colonies—the unrest that would soon be called revolution.

Evacuation

Under English rule, the free Black families of Fort Mose and Spain's Native allies were not just vulnerable—they were redefinable. What Spain had recognized in law, Britain could erase through its slave code. The residents of St. Augustine understood the stakes immediately: this was not a routine change of flags; it was a change of legal universe. For many, staying meant an almost certain return to bondage, forced removal, or violent retaliation by those who had long resented Spanish sanctuary. So St. Augustine did something rare in colonial history: it emptied itself.

Illustrated map of North America, 1763, showing Spanish, French, and English territories.

In 1763–1764, the Spanish evacuation carried just over three thousand people from St. Augustine and its hinterland to Cuba—records commonly cite 3,103 evacuees.[2] Those leaving were not only Spanish officials and soldiers, but whole households: women, children, free people of color, enslaved people, artisans, and mission-connected families. They dismantled their lives—goods packed, doors barred, gardens abandoned—and sailed for the vicinity of Matanzas, where Spain would attempt to resettle them on new land.

Francisco Menéndez went with them. The captain of Mose's militia, the man who had fought for Spanish Florida and helped make sanctuary real on the ground, joined the Fort Mose community in exile. In Cuba, they tried to recreate what they had built north of St. Augustine, forming a new settlement called San Agustín de la Nueva Florida.

Only a few stayed behind. Sources just three families chose to remain in St. Augustine after the Spanish withdrew. The handover of 1763 lands was not a footnote after a distant European war but a lived catastrophe and a calculated escape. The fort still stood. The city still stood. But the community that had defended them, prayed in them, and built a frontier life around them boarded ships and left, because the English definition of order left no room for Black sanctuary or Spanish-allied Native autonomy.

Florida: England's 14th and 15th Colonies

It was the dawn of a new British map of North America. For the first time since Spain had claimed La Florida nearly two centuries earlier, Britain could say it controlled the entire Atlantic seaboard from Nova Scotia down through the Floridas. While schoolbooks recite "the thirteen colonies" as a fixed fact, in reality it was a political snapshot taken at a single moment, and even then it was incomplete. By the 1770s, Britain's mainland colonies were not just the famous thirteen. There were fifteen, and the two most recently acquired were the ones most Americans forget. The Apalachicola River split Florida into East and West.

St. Augustine—about 300 buildings strong by then—became the capital of East Florida. The city that had survived sieges and fires was now a hollowed place—ready to be renamed, reorganized, and, in the English story that followed, largely forgotten. Pensacola became the capital of West Florida, whose jurisdiction extended westward toward the Mississippi River.

A Tale of Two Governors

When British Major James Grant arrived in East Florida in 1764, he did not inherit a thriving colony. He inherited absence. Most of the population had sailed for Cuba, leaving only three families, a fortified town, and miles of overgrown hammocks and pine barrens pressing back toward the sea. St. Augustine stood intact—its coquina walls solid, its streets laid out—but it was empty. Grant governed a map more than people.

He was a broad, heavyset man, his ruddy face flushed from the sea wind, and the red of his officer's coat cut sharply against the pale coquina walls of Castillo de San Marcos. He did not arrive as a dreamer but as a soldier with orders. His task was blunt: populate, secure, and make it pay. He had seen war in Europe and North America and understood the importance of supply lines and discipline. What he saw now was underused land and a strategic coastline—a province that could either drain the Crown or justify its acquisition.

He walked through empty streets once crowded with Spanish soldiers, Minorcan laborers, free Black militiamen, and Native allies. Most were gone—sailed to Cuba rather than live under British law. A colony without settlers was a liability. The Major with the thick Scottish accent would have to manufacture momentum. He would need to import it.

The plan was to offer generous land grants to anyone willing to settle the province. Advertisements circulated promising opportunity: fertile soil, mild winters, and a chance to start over. Investors and planters listened. Grant also brought his own enslaved laborers, trained in the refinements of French cuisine and wine service, and he staged elaborate dinners. Visitors wrote about the hospitality, the tables heavy with food and drink, the cultivated air of civility in what was otherwise a frontier outpost.[3] The revelry was strategic, and it worked.

Portrait of James Grant, Public Domain

Speculators arrived, as did planters from the Carolinas and the West Indies. They brought capital, surveyors, and more enslaved Africans. Along the Atlantic coast and upriver from St. Augustine, plantations began to take shape—indigo first, then rice and other export crops. The British system was not defensive like Spain's. It was extractive and expansionist by design. Land was cleared quickly, requiring more labor. Roads were cut, swamps drained, and survey lines were run through forests that had once buffered Spanish missions and Native settlements. Unlike Spanish Florida's more fluid legal categories, British law codified chattel slavery—hereditary, racial, and absolute.

The frontier shifted from a mixed military outpost to an agricultural enterprise. Profit replaced persistence as the organizing principle. Where Spain had subsidized Florida as a strategic cost, Britain intended to make it profitable.

The contrast between the Spanish governors who had defended St. Augustine and the British governor who sought to populate it is stark. Under Spain, Florida survived through stone walls, royal subsidies, and negotiated alliances with Native nations and free Black communities. Under Grant, survival meant economic transformation: investor dinners, imported enslaved labor, and the steady imposition of plantation discipline. One system endured by resisting expansion; the other aimed to expand or fail.

Within a decade of the British takeover, the landscape itself began to change. The scrub and marsh gave way to fields worked by enslaved hands. The revelry at St. Augustine's governor's residence masked a harsher reality beyond its walls. What had once been a borderland defined by sanctuary and militia duty was becoming part of the broader southern slave economy.

West Florida: Experiment and Collapse

If East Florida under James Grant was a calculated plantation experiment, West Florida presented a different kind of instability. Centered in Pensacola, it was newer, sparser, and more volatile. It was bordered by Creek, Choctaw, and Chickasaw lands and dependent on those fragile alliances. British authority there was less about refinement and recruitment dinners and more about negotiation, trade, and constant vigilance. The population was sparse, infrastructure limited, and the promise of prosperity louder than the reality.

Into that uncertainty stepped British General Patrick Tonyn with the posture of a career officer—lean, sharp-faced, and disciplined. His powdered hair was set in the fashion of the day, his coat dark and formal, his bearing controlled. Where Grant had surveyed vacancy and possibility, Tonyn surveyed instability.

Tonyn was from an English border town that had known centuries of shifting allegiance between England and Scotland. He was born into uniform. His father, Charles Tonyn, was a colonel in the 6th (Inniskilling) Dragoons, and military discipline was less a career choice than a family inheritance.

Tonyn entered the 6th Dragoons and rose to captain in 1751. He learned soldiering not in theory but on Europe's proving ground. During the Seven Years' War, he served in Germany, where Britain's continental campaigns demanded coordination, endurance, and nerve. In 1759, his regiment fought at the Battle of Minden and later at

Wetter—engagements remembered for disciplined infantry standing against cavalry and artillery under punishing conditions. Promotions followed.

Under Tonyn's governorship, East Florida avoided the kind of sustained frontier war that had plagued earlier decades. That stability owed much to his relationship with Ahaya the Cowkeeper, the influential leader of the Seminole Alachua band.

Ahaya—often called "the Cowkeeper" by the British because of the large herds of cattle his people managed in north-central Florida—was a pragmatic diplomat. His band controlled critical interior routes and grazing lands between the St. Johns River and the Gulf approaches. Tonyn understood that holding East Florida during the Revolutionary era required more than troops; it required Indigenous neutrality or alliance. Through trade, recognition of territorial boundaries, and steady diplomacy, Tonyn maintained a working peace with Ahaya.

The arrangement was mutually beneficial. The Seminoles benefited from regulated trade and a British counterweight against rival Native groups and encroaching settlers. The British benefited from intelligence, stability in the interior, and the avoidance of a two-front conflict while revolution burned to the north.[4] In a period defined by shifting loyalties and imperial collapse, Tonyn's steady relationship with Ahaya helped keep East Florida comparatively calm—at least until diplomacy in Europe once again reshaped the province's fate.

Portrait of Patrick Tonyn, Public Domain

Competing with Tonyn's steady hand was Dr. Andrew Turbnull. He did not arrive in Florida with a royal commission but with a contract.

Turnbull was a Scottish physician turned colonial speculator, married into Mediterranean networks, and fluent in the language of opportunity. Where Governor Grant saw empty acreage needing settlers, Turnbull saw a grand experiment: import labor from the Old World and build a profitable colony from the ground up. He persuaded powerful investors in London and secured one of the largest land grants in British East Florida — more than 100,000 acres south of St. Augustine along the Mosquito Coast. On paper, it was visionary. In practice, it would become infamous.

Turnbull recruited more than a thousand indentured laborers from Minorca, Greece, and Italy, promising them land and prosperity upon completion of their service. He named the settlement New Smyrna after his wife's birthplace in the Mediterranean. But this was not a refuge; it was a plantation colony designed to produce indigo and other export crops for Atlantic markets.

He arrived as a planner and proprietor, not a soldier. Yet what he attempted demanded the discipline of an army and the endurance of a frontier garrison. The wilderness was harsher than advertised. Disease spread quickly, and supplies ran thin. Contracts that looked orderly in London felt punishing in the Florida heat. What began as Britain's boldest immigration venture in East Florida would test the limits of indenture — and expose how thin the line could be between contract labor and coercion.

Turnbull believed he was building a model colony. Instead, New Smyrna became a cautionary tale — one that compelled Governor Patrick Tonyn to intervene and reshaped East Florida's population for decades.

Three times the size of Jamestown, New Smyrna promised land and opportunity after a term of service. What the laborers encountered instead was brutal discipline, disease, and isolation. Though legally indentured rather than enslaved, many later described conditions indistinguishable from bondage. Mortality was staggering, starvation and beatings were common, and complaints were ignored.

Servants fled in increasing numbers. Some died in the swamps trying to reach St. Augustine. Others endured until 1777, when nearly 600 survivors marched to the capital and petitioned Governor Patrick Tonyn directly.[5] Tonyn, who had his own conflicts with plantation elites and political rivals, intervened decisively. He declared that Turnbull had violated the terms of indenture, effectively treating European laborers as enslaved chattel. The New Smyrna plantation was dissolved, the laborers were released from their contracts, and resettled in St. Augustine.

The episode exposed the fault lines of British Florida. Grant had built East Florida on plantation logic and enslaved African labor. Turnbull tried to replicate plantation discipline with European indentured servants but collapsed under abuse and mismanagement. Tonyn's intervention was not humanitarian idealism but governance. A colony that could not regulate its own labor system risked rebellion, scandal, and economic failure.

By the eve of the American Revolution, British Florida was a place of contradiction. It was expanding, yes—new plantations, new trade, and new immigration. But it was also unstable: dependent on enslaved labor, vulnerable to escape and unrest, politically divided, and surrounded by

Native nations whose alliances were strategic, not guaranteed. The British had acquired Florida to complete their Atlantic map. Governing it proved far more complicated than coloring it red.

❖

Revolution Comes to Florida

When rebellion erupted in the older mainland colonies, Florida stood apart. It was newly British, tightly managed, and populated by people who had arrived only yesterday rather than generations earlier. East and West Florida had been carved into royal colonies in 1763 and were governed with a firmer hand than the long-settled provinces to the north. There were no deep-rooted assemblies with decades of precedent, no entrenched political class accustomed to self-rule.

Residents were recent immigrants, land-seekers, soldiers, merchants, displaced Loyalists, and plantation investors. They hadn't spent their lives arguing with London. They had come because London offered land, protection, and opportunity. So when revolutionary grievances about taxation, representation, and imperial overreach began to spread, Florida did not respond with the same reflex. These colonies remained loyal to the Crown.

That loyalty mattered because geography mattered. It was contested by Spain, harried by patriot raids, used as a

base for British operations, and fought over along the
Mississippi and the Gulf.

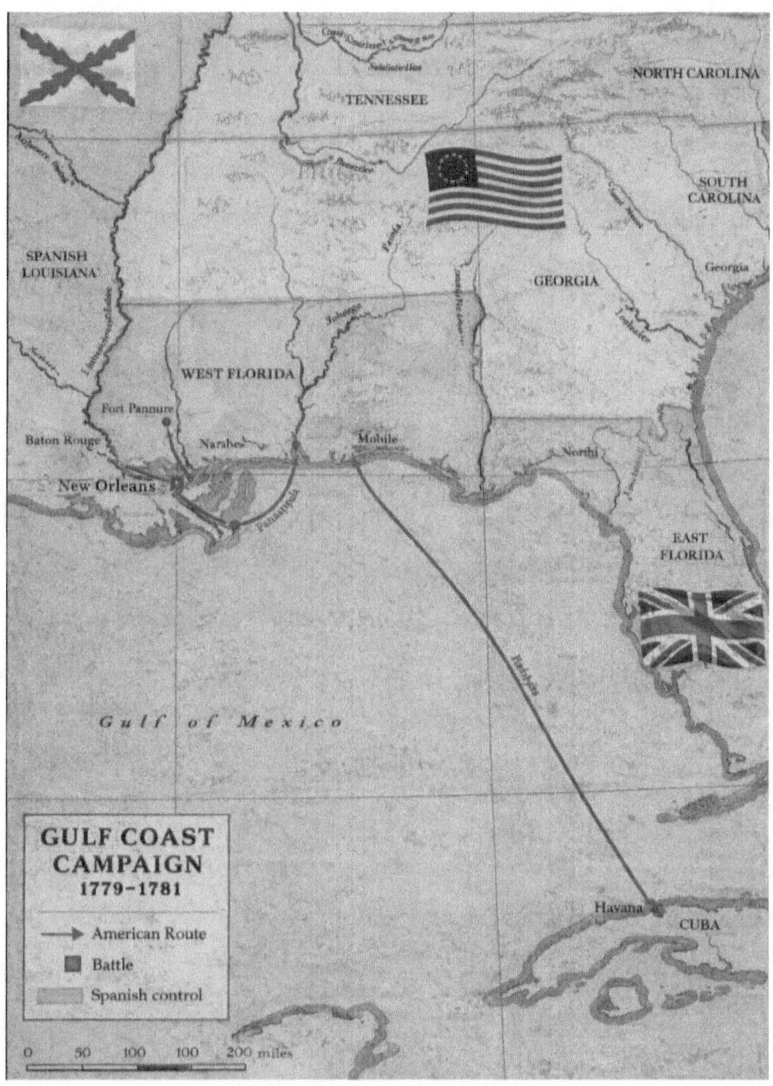

Illustration Map of Gulf Coast Campaign

East Florida's capital, St. Augustine, anchored the
Atlantic flank; West Florida, with Pensacola as its capital,
guarded the Gulf and the river routes feeding the

153

continent's interior. Whoever controlled the Floridas could threaten or protect the Mississippi corridor and the Gulf coast. The Revolution was never just a war of New England town greens. It was a contest for supply lines, ports, and waterways—and Florida sat on the edge of all of them.

During the early years of the conflict, both sides needed the artery of the Mississippi River. Troop movements, trade, intelligence, and influence flowed through it. Skirmishes and raids flared along the lower river and its tributaries. Forts changed hands. Small battles carried outsized consequences because they determined who could move goods and troops through the interior. On the Gulf, Pensacola became both a prize and a base—protected by British fortifications but vulnerable to Spanish attack once Spain entered the war against Britain in 1779.

In the east, St. Augustine became a Loyalist refuge. As patriots seized power along the coast, thousands loyal to Britain fled not only north to Canada but also south into Florida. The town swelled with refugees, including officials, planters, merchants, and families who had lost property and safety in the rebellious colonies.

Florida's war was often less about set-piece battles than about containment: raids across the Georgia border, privateering along the coast, intelligence networks, and the constant pressure of frontier warfare. The Castillo still stood, but the threat now came from a different direction—from a continent splitting into rival allegiances.

Spain didn't just cheer from the sidelines. It fed the war. Spanish forces worked to unravel the British grip, funneling money, gunpowder, arms, and medical supplies to the rebels through a shadow network that ran through New Orleans, Havana, and Spanish merchants in Europe. After Bernardo de Gálvez became governor of New Orleans in 1777, shipments of muskets, uniforms, and cash moved up the Mississippi into the American interior, where Washington's army and frontier forces were perpetually short.

Then Spain made it official. In June 1779, Spain declared war on Britain and opened a second major theater of war: the Gulf Coast campaign.[6] This is the part most Revolution narratives strip out. While Washington fought in the East, Spain went after Britain's southern underbelly—Baton Rouge, Mobile, and finally Pensacola—forcing Britain to defend its Gulf flank instead of using it to squeeze the rebels.

Spanish ships also carried something else the British found intolerable: free Black troops. Organized companies within Spain's imperial forces included free Black men who served openly in uniform under the Spanish flag. In Gálvez's campaigns, these units fought as part of the assault forces. Their very presence undercut Britain's racial order just as surely as Spanish sanctuary had done in Florida decades earlier.

Pensacola was the keystone. It was the British capital of West Florida and the best deep-water base on the Gulf. If

Britain held it securely, it could threaten New Orleans, pressure the lower Mississippi, and project power into the Gulf—exactly the kind of alternate attack line that would have complicated the American war effort.

Siege of Pensacola

Spain's commander, Bernardo de Gálvez, was a young governor who understood what the Continental Congress could barely afford to admit: the American Revolution was not only a rebellion. It was a global war.

For weeks in March and April 1781, cannon fire had been shaking the trees and shorelines. Spanish ships fought their way past the narrow mouth of Pensacola Bay under relentless British fire. At one point, after his naval commanders hesitated to enter the harbor, Gálvez is said to have sailed his own vessel forward alone, daring the rest to follow. It was bravado, yes—but also calculation.[7] If Pensacola fell, Britain's hold on the Gulf would collapse.

On May 8, a Spanish shell struck the British powder magazine at Fort George, and within days, General John Campbell surrendered to Bernardo de Gálvez. The Siege of Pensacola ran from March 9 to May 10, 1781—a two-month grind of landings, trench work, artillery, and attrition—until British defenses collapsed, West Florida fell, and the British lost their final foothold on the Gulf Coast.

That victory didn't win the Revolution by itself, but it changed the geometry of the war. With Gulf Coast pressure and Pensacola gone, Britain's southern strategy lost a critical base and a major avenue for attack and resupply. Spain had helped pin Britain in place—first with money and materiel, then with force—so the war didn't become a two-front disaster for the Americans.

Illustration, Gulf Coast Campaign

Florida's Revolution, then, is not a footnote to the "thirteen colonies." It is the missing flank. The American Revolution did not simply unfold around Florida. Florida was inside it—caught between empires again, as it had been for two centuries, its fate shaped less by slogans than by ships, rivers, and the hard logic of geography.

1784, Spanish Florida (Again)

When the war ended in 1783, Britain ceded East and West Florida to Spain as part of a broader peace settlement. Florida had been British for only about twenty years, a colonial regime barely old enough to take root before it was uprooted again.

The handover didn't happen overnight. The change of flags triggered another forced migration; this time, British officials and many Loyalist settlers had to leave, and evacuations continued into the mid-1780s. They went to the Bahamas, Jamaica, and other British possessions—carrying with them their losses, claims, and, often, the people they enslaved. Historians estimate that roughly 14,000–15,000 Loyalist emigrants (and the enslaved people they brought) either passed through or ultimately left from East Florida during the evacuation period. They spread across the province, settling undeveloped stretches of the St. Johns, the Mosquito/Inlet region, and plantation tracts along the coast.

Meanwhile, some of the Spanish-era residents who had gone into exile in 1763 returned from Cuba once Spain regained the province—though the "Second Spanish Period" population was now a mix of returnees and newer English, Minorcan, and American families. But the town Spain reclaimed was not the Spanish town it had lost in 1763.

Spain's problem was not a new one: the maps looked impressive, but the state's capacity did not. Madrid wanted productive agriculture and stable frontier control, but late-eighteenth-century Spain was stretched thin by wars and imperial expenses. Florida stayed under-resourced, dependent on garrisons, local improvisation, and the fragile glue of trade and diplomacy.

On the ground, power in the interior flowed through Native politics and commerce. The Seminole world that had developed in Florida in the eighteenth century did not vanish with the change of flags. Leaders such as Ahaya ("Cowkeeper") had anchored the Alachua region during the British years; after his death in the mid-1780s, Spain sought to stabilize relations rather than fight a costly frontier war it could not afford.

Illustration, Ahaya "Cowkeeper"

Meanwhile, the United States continued to expand southward in both population and ambition. Florida was no longer the old Spanish frontier facing only Britain. Now a new United States pressed from the north, Spanish Louisiana (and shifting French interests) from the west, and a Gulf-Caribbean world still shaped by imperial war and trade. Spanish officials in St. Augustine and Pensacola reoccupied forts, rebuilt administration, and tried to reassert authority over a province that was underpopulated, cash-poor, and strategically exposed.

Throughout the 1780s and early 1790s, Florida was both a border and a temptation—an adjacent imperial possession whose boundaries and ports mattered to American settlers and merchants alike.

For enslaved people in Georgia and the Carolinas, the change of flags revived an old hope: Florida had once been a door out of slavery. In the late 1600s and early 1700s, Spanish sanctuary policy had offered freedom to fugitives who reached Florida, converted, and served the Crown. Even after Spain returned in 1784, enslaved people continued to run south, often aiming not just for Spanish officials but for refuge among Native communities in the interior.

But the diplomatic reality had changed. Spain was now dealing with an independent United States that demanded cooperation on borders, trade, and "property," including enslaved people.

It was Thomas Jefferson who finally ended Spain's policy of sheltering runaways. As Secretary of State, he personally pressed Spanish officials to stop treating Florida as a refuge for enslaved people escaping from the United States, framing sanctuary as an intolerable threat to American "property" and border stability.[8] Spain yielded: in May 1790, King Charles IV issued an edict withdrawing the century-old sanctuary policy that had once made Florida a beacon for fugitives.

The result was a Florida full of contradictions: Spanish again, yet steadily constrained by U.S. demands; still a place people fled toward, yet no longer one that could openly promise them freedom; a slave society itself, even as its interior—especially in Seminole country—remained a zone where escape and re-enslavement collided.

By 1800, St. Augustine had become what it would remain for the rest of Spain's second tenure: a small, strategic town in a widening Atlantic world. Spanish again, but never purely Spanish; a place held together by forts, families who had learned to survive regime change, and the constant awareness that the next transfer might already be forming somewhere else—on a diplomat's desk, on a surveyor's chain, or on a frontier road leading south.

[1] Gayarré, Charles (1867). History of Louisiana : The Spanish domination, Volume 3. New York: Widdleton.

[2] Florida Museum of Natural History, "Exodus (1763–1764)," St. Augustine: A Brief History, University of Florida.

[3] Hill, James L. (Fall 2014). "New Systems, Established Traditions: Governor James Grant's Indian Diplomacy and the Evolution of British Colonial Policy, 1760-1771". The Florida Historical Quarterly.

[4] Patrick Tonyn: Britain's Most Effective Revolutionary-Era Royal Governor". Journal of the American Revolution.

[5] LANE, MARCIA. "Oldest city was loyal to the crown". The St. Augustine Record.

[6] Worcester, Donald E. (1967). "Review of Spain's Final Triumph over Great Britain in the Gulf of Mexico: The Battle of Pensacola, March 9 to May 8, 1781". The American Historical Review.

[7] N. Orwin Rush (1966). Spain's Final Triumph Over Great Britain in the Gulf of Mexico: The Battle of Pensacola March 9 to May 8, 1781. Florida State University.

[8] R. K. Murdoch, "The Return of Runaway Slaves, 1790–1794," The Florida Historical Quarterly 44, no. 1 (1965).

7

1800-1900

Those who deny freedom to others, deserve it not for themselves;
and, under a just God, can not long retain it.

— Abraham Lincoln

THE RIVER WAS THE line between worlds.

They reached it at dusk, mud to their knees, dogs somewhere behind them, and the current in front of them black and slow. The St. Marys River was not just water—it was an international boundary. On one bank lay Georgia, where slave patrols carried federal warrants and planter authority. On the other lay Spanish Florida, thinly governed and thick with rumor. The people heading towards it did not know the details about treaties or dates; they only knew that south meant possibility. They slipped into the water.

Perilous Journeys

By 1800, enslaved people from the American colonies were still running. Spain had formally withdrawn its old sanctuary edict in 1790, but the borderlands did not operate on decrees alone. Enslaved men and women fled toward the interior swamps and pine barrens, seeking refuge no longer with Spanish officials in St. Augustine but with Seminole communities in the backwoods. There, a distinct network of Black settlements, often called "Black Seminoles" in later records, took root in uneasy alliance with Native bands. Freedom was negotiated, defended, and conditional. But it existed.

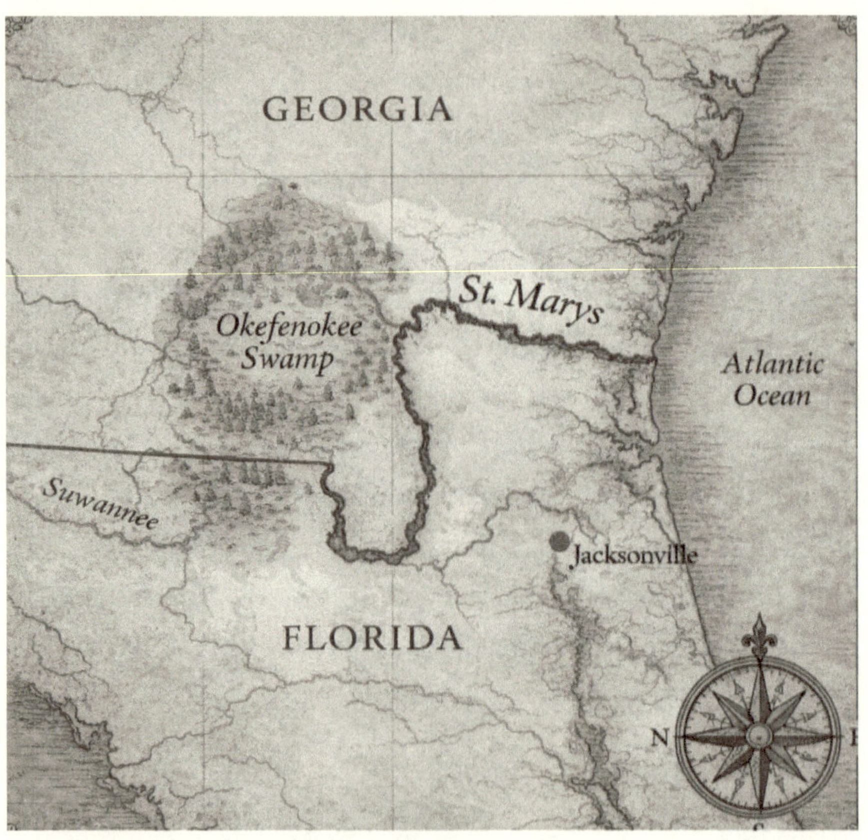

Illustration St. Marys River

The St. Marys River, today the quiet border between Georgia and Florida, was then a geopolitical seam. It divided the United States from Spain. It also divided the slave code from ambiguity. Raids crossed it frequently, Georgia militia units pursued fugitives into Florida, and Florida-based fighters and Seminole allies retaliated. Cattle were stolen. Plantations burned. People were seized and re-seized. The period between 1800 and 1821 was not orderly frontier expansion. It was lawless and combustible, shaped by vigilantes as much as governors.

Border Battles

Meanwhile, empires shifted again. In 1800, Spain returned Louisiana to France. Three years later, the United States purchased Louisiana, suddenly extending American territory west of Florida to the Mississippi and beyond. Florida, once a flank of Spain's continental empire, now found itself hemmed in—American territory to the north and west, the Gulf and the Atlantic to the south and east. It was increasingly isolated, increasingly pressured, and increasingly difficult for Spain to defend.

That isolation mattered. Florida became less a colony than a corridor for smugglers, runaways, Native alliances, and American expansionists impatient with Spanish sovereignty. Spain tried to maintain neutrality and avoid war, but it lacked troops and funds. The interior remained a negotiated space, where Seminole leaders and Black communities maintained autonomy neither Spain nor the United States fully controlled.

But in those early years, before formal annexation and before the Seminole Wars hardened lines, it was still a place where a man could reach a river at dusk and gamble everything on crossing it.

❖

The Patriot War (1812-1813)

In 1812, as the United States edged toward war with Britain over maritime trade restrictions, anxiety spread along the southern frontier. Washington feared that Britain, which had aligned diplomatically with Spain during the Napoleonic upheavals, might use Spanish Florida as a staging ground. St. Augustine, still under Spanish control, lay uncomfortably close to Georgia's plantations and Atlantic shipping lanes. Rather than declare war on Spain outright, American expansionists sought a workaround.

What followed became known as the Patriot War.[1] A force of so-called "Patriots" moved into East Florida with the goal of forcing Spanish authority out and paving the way for American annexation. Comprised of Georgia militiamen and local adventurers, and quietly supported by U.S. officials, they seized Amelia Island, raising a flag of "republican" rebellion while U.S. naval vessels hovered offshore. The plan was to move south and pressure St. Augustine into submission.

But President James Madison, wary of provoking a broader conflict with Spain while the United States was preparing for war with Britain, hesitated. Officially, American troops were instructed to occupy strategic positions but avoid overt conquest. Inside the Castillo de San Marcos, Spanish officials received similar orders: hold position, avoid escalation, and do not fire first. For weeks, East Florida remained in uneasy paralysis—a war without declaration, a siege without assault.

Outside the walls, the restraint frayed. Patriot forces and irregular fighters looted plantations, burned property, and destabilized the countryside. St. Augustine once again endured destruction in its orbit, but this time the violence was not confined to one side. Seminole bands and Black fighters retaliated across the border into Georgia, attacking northern plantations, destroying property, and liberating enslaved people. Florida's interior became a moving frontier of raid and counter-raid.

Among the defenders of St. Augustine were approximately sixty free Black men, some of them recent runaways from Georgia. Led by figures like Juan Bautista (often called "Prince William" or "Big Prince"), they fought alongside Seminole allies.

At Twelve Mile Swamp, these combined forces ambushed Patriot troops, forcing them into retreat. The encounter was small by conventional military standards, but symbolically potent: Black and Native fighters defending Spanish Florida against American irregulars.

American newspapers responded predictably, casting the Seminole and Black resistance as savage aggression rather than organized defense. Editorials condemned what they described as "Indian and Negro depredations," reinforcing a racialized narrative that framed frontier violence as proof of lawlessness south of the border. The language helped build public support for stronger intervention.

Four years later, another conflict erupted. In July 1816, U.S. forces destroyed the "Negro Fort" on the Apalachicola River, which had been occupied by free Black fighters and allied Seminoles. The explosion that followed the American bombardment killed more than 250 people inside. To southern planters, the fort represented a direct threat: an armed refuge for freedom seekers on the edge of slave territory. Its destruction marked the opening salvo of what would become the First Seminole War.

First Seminole War, 1818

In March 1818, Andrew Jackson gathered his army at Fort Scott—eight hundred regulars in blue, two thousand Tennessee and Georgia volunteers, and nearly fourteen hundred Lower Creek warriors. They were bound not for a battlefield but for Spanish Florida. The line between pursuit and invasion would be drawn later, but for now, it was a column of men moving south.

On March 15, Jackson's force crossed into Florida and followed the bends of the Apalachicola River. They turned toward the Mikasuki towns clustered around Lake Miccosukee. On March 31, Anhaica, near present-day

Tallahassee, was burned. The next day, Miccosukee fell. More than three hundred homes were reduced to ash; villages erased. The destruction was swift, almost administrative. His forces then moved through Creek, Seminole, and Miccosukee settlements across northern Florida, burning them to the ground. The campaign was not limited to Native communities; it also targeted Black Seminoles and allied maroon settlements that had formed in the borderlands.

Maroons, Mechanical Curator collection, Public Domain.

By April 6, Jackson stood before Fort St. Marks, Spain's weathered Gulf outpost. He wrote to the commandant, Don Francisco Caso y Luengo, explaining that he had entered Florida on presidential orders. He claimed that the wife of Chief Chennabee had confessed that the Seminoles had taken ammunition from the Spanish fort with the intent to attack. On the "principle of self-defense," Jackson insisted that American troops would need to occupy St. Marks to prevent further aid to his enemies. He styled himself a "Friend of Spain."

Luengo replied cautiously. He denied the charge. The Seminoles, he said, had neither taken possession of the fort nor drawn on its stores. He worried aloud about the consequences of admitting American troops without Madrid's approval. It did not matter. On April 7, Jackson seized the fort anyway.

Inside, he found two men who, in American eyes, embodied foreign meddling: Alexander George Arbuthnot, a Scottish merchant, and Robert Ambrister, a former British officer who had drifted into Florida's borderland intrigues. Rumor said they armed the Indians and whispered of British support. In truth, trade and politics were inseparable on this frontier; a gun could be both livelihood and leverage. Jackson arrested Arbuthnot on the spot, but let Ambrister go for the time being.

Next came two Red Stick Creek leaders who had allied themselves with Seminole/Mikasuki resistance networks that were caught in Jackson's ire.

Hillis Hadjo, "Josiah Francis," was a Red Stick prophet who had once traveled to London seeking British recognition. Homathlemico was a Creek war leader linked to the recent violence along the Georgia frontier. Together, they were lured out to an American vessel flying the Union Jack near St. Marks. In this borderland, flags were a language. A British ensign suggested parley, perhaps protection. Instead, it was a trap. They were seized and brought ashore under guard.

Hillis Hadjo and Homathlemico taken captive

At Fort San Marcos de Apalache, there was no formal hearing, tribunal, or exchange of testimony. Jackson considered them instigators of the war—men who had stirred resistance among Red Sticks, Seminoles, and Black allies and, in his view, bore responsibility for frontier killings. But he did not convene a court. He ordered them hanged. Homathlemico was executed first; Francis followed shortly after. The rope settled the matter more quickly than due process.

The act was more than retribution. It was a statement. Spain still claimed Florida. Britain still cast a shadow across the Gulf. Native towns still resisted. By hanging the leaders at a Spanish fort he had just seized, Jackson collapsed those sovereignties into his own. Territory could be invaded; forts occupied; and foreign subjects tried. Native leaders—captured under a foreign flag—could be executed without civil process. The frontier was no longer simply contested ground. It was becoming an American frontier, defined by force first and paperwork later.

Jackson pressed on toward the Suwannee River, where Maroons—free Black fighters who had fled the destruction of the Negro Fort—had regrouped at Bowlegs Town under a Black Seminole leader named Nero. Their presence was another rebuke: armed, organized, and beyond the reach of American slave codes. They were, in many ways, the true target.

On April 12, along the Econfina River, Jackson's forces and their Creek allies struck a Red Stick village, killing dozens and taking women and children captive. At Bowlegs Town, resistance flickered and then fled. Jackson occupied the settlement overnight. In the darkness, former British officer Ambrister wandered into the American camp, believing it still friendly ground. This time, he was arrested. With Black resistance broken and the principal Seminole towns destroyed, Jackson declared victory. He dismissed the Georgia militia and the Lower Creeks and marched back to St. Marks with his two British prisoners.

There, a military tribunal convened. Arbuthnot and Ambrister were charged with inciting the Seminoles and Spanish against the United States—foreign hands stirring a frontier war. The court sentenced both to death, then reconsidered, commuting Ambrister's sentence to lashes and hard labor. Jackson overruled them.[2] On April 29, 1818, Ambrister faced a firing squad. Arbuthnot was hanged from the yardarm of his own ship.

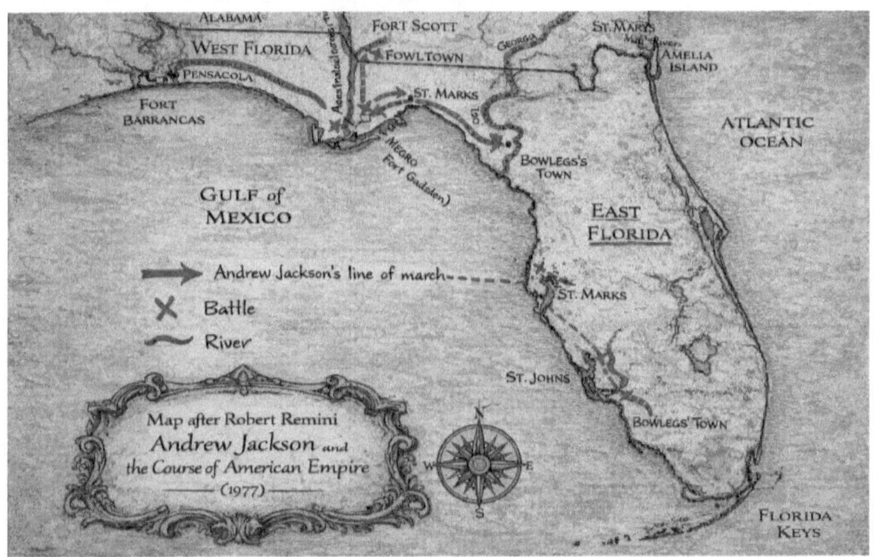

Map of Jackson's Movements during Seminole War

The executions sent tremors through Washington and London. Jackson had invaded Spanish territory, occupied a foreign fort, executed British subjects, and hanged Native leaders without a civil trial—all in the name of security. He left a garrison at St. Marks and returned to Fort Gadsden, reporting that peace had been restored and that he would soon head home to Nashville.

But peace was not what he had secured. He had exposed Spain's weakness in Florida and shown that American power could outrun its own laws. The frontier had shifted, not only on the ground but in the meaning of American force. The larger truth was becoming undeniable: Spain no longer had the troops, money, or administrative reach to control Florida's interior.

❖

1821–1835: The Uneasy American Florida

Across the ocean, Spain was collapsing. No longer an empire capable of defending its overseas territories, it had lost Argentina, Peru, and Mexico and was no longer a dominant European power. The result was a diplomatic rather than a military surrender.

Under the Adams–Onís Treaty, signed in 1819 and implemented in 1821, Spain ceded Florida to the United States for the final time. In exchange, the United States renounced its claims to Texas and fixed the boundary along the Sabine River. Florida passed from Spain to the United States not through a decisive battlefield victory but through accumulated instability—border violence, slave flight, Native resistance, and American military pressure.

On paper, that transfer looked orderly. Flags lowered, papers signed, and officials changed desks again. But the ground beneath those desks had never settled. American authorities inherited a landscape Spain had struggled for decades to control: Seminole towns scattered across northern and central Florida, Black Seminole settlements interwoven among them, former maroon communities still remembered in planter nightmares, and a border population accustomed to ignoring distant governments. The U.S. did not inherit peace. It inherited unfinished business and tried to do what bureaucrats do best: reorganize it.

The Treaty of Moultrie Creek (1823) was intended as a step toward structure. Seminoles were required to relocate from northern Florida to a designated reservation in the peninsula's interior. In theory, this separated them from American settlers and from enslaved populations near the Georgia border. In practice, it compressed communities onto less fertile land and formalized American expectations of surveillance. U.S. forts rose along the coasts and interior corridors — not just for protection but as pressure points.

What had once been a contested imperial territory became a bureaucratically managed American frontier. Or so it seemed. In reality, the tensions that had drawn Jackson south would resurface within a decade in the far more brutal Second Seminole War.

The Black Seminole question remained the explosive core. Southern slaveholders believed that Black communities living among Seminoles were stolen property. They demanded the return of fugitives. Seminole leaders resisted being forced into the role of slave catchers. The federal government attempted to craft a compromise — distinguishing between "negroes" owned by Seminoles and those claimed by American planters — but on the ground, those categories blurred. Kinship, alliance, and shared defense mattered more than paperwork.

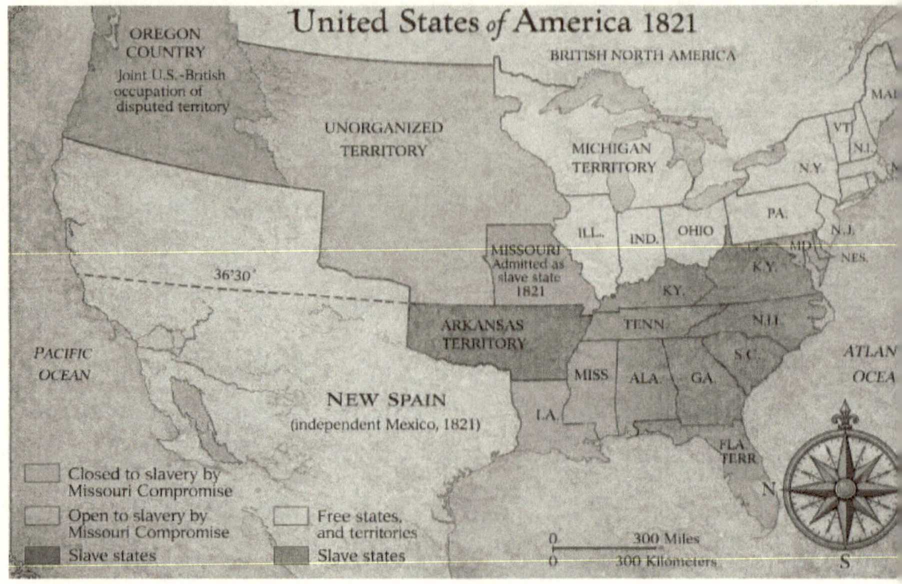

Illustration, Map of the United States, 1821

Meanwhile, American settlement accelerated. Cotton culture pushed south, and planters eyed Florida's soil while speculators eyed its ports. The same expansionist logic that had swallowed Georgia and Alabama now turned toward the peninsula. Florida was no longer a buffer zone between empires. It was a target for national growth.

Indian Removal Act, 1830

America's focus now turned to the problem of Native Americans who had called the region home for more than 12,000 years. What had been a negotiated reservation in 1823 was only temporary. The focus now was to remove

Native populations permanently west of the Mississippi. Seminole leaders, including younger figures who would soon emerge as central voices of resistance, recognized the shift immediately. The reservation was not protection. It was a waiting room.

The Removal Order

By 1830, the debate in Washington had narrowed to a single question: would Native nations remain within expanding American states or be relocated? President Andrew Jackson answered with policy. The Indian Removal Act authorized the federal government to negotiate land-exchange treaties, trading Indigenous homelands in the Southeast for territory in what was then called Indian Territory (present-day Oklahoma). Officially, removal was framed as voluntary and protective. In practice, it relied on pressure, coercion, and the implicit threat of force.

The law primarily targeted the so-called "Five Civilized Tribes" of the Deep South: Cherokee, Creek, Choctaw, Chickasaw, and Seminole. These nations had adopted elements of Anglo-American governance and agriculture but retained their political sovereignty and land claims. The Choctaw were among the first forced west between 1831 and 1833; thousands died along the way. The Creek followed. The Cherokee removal in 1838–1839 — remembered as the Trail of Tears — became the most widely known, with roughly 16,000 people driven west and thousands dying from exposure, disease, and starvation.[3]

Florida's situation was different—and combustible. The Seminoles were not a centralized nation with a single capital to seize; they were a confederation of towns spread across swamps and forests, interwoven with Black Seminole communities. The 1823 Treaty of Moultrie Creek had already confined them to a reservation in central Florida. For Native families, removal meant more than relocation. It meant severing ties to hunting grounds, cattle ranges, burial sites, and alliances built over generations. It meant leaving terrain that offered natural defenses— marsh, hammock, and river—for unfamiliar plains. More than an administrative adjustment, removal was a demographic upheaval that uprooted entire nations.

It also meant abandoning Black allies who risked re-enslavement if separated. For American slaveholders, removal promised something else: the collapse of a refuge system that had long unsettled the southern plantation economy.

In Florida, the attempt to apply the Removal Act collided with a landscape and a people unwilling to quietly disappear into the margins of a growing republic. When federal agents and soldiers began enforcing removal in the mid-1830s, resistance hardened. Some Seminole bands prepared to migrate under duress, while others refused outright. Tensions over disputed slave claims, treaty legitimacy, and U.S. military pressure escalated, and by 1835, the pressure snapped.

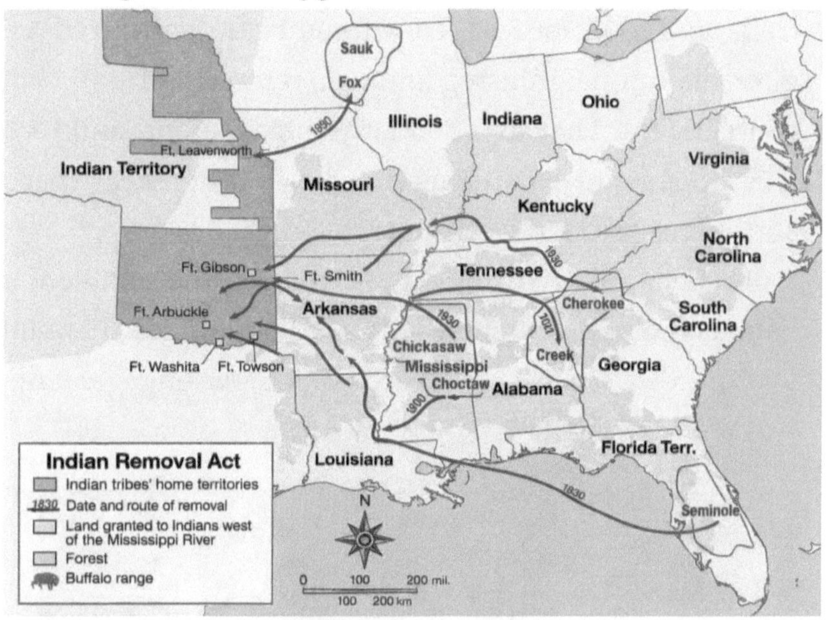

Map, 1830 Indian Removal Act

Second Seminole War, 1835

In December, Major Francis Dade and more than 100 U.S. soldiers were ambushed by local tribes while marching between forts in central Florida. Only a handful survived. The attack signaled that removal would not proceed quietly. What followed was the Second Seminole War, a grinding conflict that stretched from northern Florida's peninsula through the Everglades and even into the Florida Keys.

The Seminoles were outnumbered and outgunned. At its height, the United States deployed more than 30,000 regular troops, militia, and volunteers in Florida. Seminole leaders turned geography into a weapon. They knew the peninsula's waterways, seasonal flood patterns, hidden trails, and food sources. They fought a decentralized guerrilla campaign using ambush, retreat, and concealment. They avoided large engagements and forced U.S. troops into exhausting marches through heat, insects, and disease-ridden wetlands.

The U.S. Army struggled to pin down the small, mobile bands who struck their supply lines and forced them into a war of exhaustion. There were no decisive engagements; it was a war of attrition.

A 20th-century McBarron illustration of U.S. Army troops with a Seminole guide. Public Domain

In 1836, General Thomas Sidney Jesup took command and shifted strategy. Rather than chasing elusive fighters, Jesup targeted the Seminoles' means of survival. He burned villages, destroyed crops, and seized cattle. Entire communities were dismantled. The goal was not battlefield victory but starvation and surrender, and the strategy expanded to include aggressive detention tactics. Jesup authorized the capture of leaders under a flag of truce, including Osceola and Micanopy in 1837—an act widely criticized at the time as a violation of wartime norms. Jesup would spend years defending the decision.

By the early 1840s, the cumulative effect of scorched-earth tactics, imprisonment, and forced transport broke much of the resistance. Thousands of Seminoles were killed, captured, or compelled to surrender and were removed west to Indian Territory. But Seminole leaders such as Osceola and John Horse rejected the removal demands.[4] Rather than assemble for transport west, several hundred natives withdrew into Florida's swamps, disappearing into the marshes and wetlands.

When active campaigning wound down in 1842, only a few hundred Seminoles remained—isolated yet unextinguished. They had not surrendered; they had endured. Their descendants form today's Seminole Tribe of Florida, headquartered in Hollywood, Florida, and the Seminole Nation of Oklahoma, based in Wewoka, Oklahoma. The Florida Seminoles are the only major Southeastern tribe that never signed a formal peace treaty with the United States. Their persistence is not folklore. It is demographic fact. Despite removal, starvation campaigns, and overwhelming military force, a remnant remained in Florida—and from that remnant, a modern sovereign tribal nation continues.

Illustration, John Horse

The Second and Third Seminole wars lasted until 1858 and became the longest and among the most expensive Indian wars in U.S. history. Roughly 1,500 American soldiers died, mostly from disease. It cost the United States

182

tens of millions of dollars and reshaped Florida permanently. By 1860, most of Florida's s tribes were nearly extinct.

Illustration, Osceola

Florida Statehood, 1845

On March 3, 1845, Florida became America's 27th state. It was now economically and politically aligned with the slave South. Almost half the state's population were enslaved African Americans working on large cotton and sugar plantations between the Apalachicola and Suwannee rivers in the north central part of the state.

Secession, 1861

Following Abraham Lincoln's election in 1860, Florida joined other Southern states in seceding from the Union and became one of the seven founding states of the Confederate States of America in 1861.

In St. Augustine, Confederates seized the old Spanish fort—the Castillo de San Marcos, then known as Fort Marion—but the gesture was short-lived. In March 1862, as Union naval power tightened its grip along the Atlantic coast, Confederate forces quietly withdrew. Federal ships entered the harbor, and the Stars and Stripes flew over the coquina walls without a battle.

St. Augustine did not burn. No great armies clashed in its streets. Instead, the war settled into something quieter and more transformative. The city became a Union outpost—part garrison, part supply station, part symbol of federal reach into the Deep South. From its harbor, blockading vessels watched the coast. Within its walls, soldiers occupied the same fort Spain had built to defend its empire. The town endured occupation for most of the war, spared the devastation of major combat, yet not untouched by the conflict's slow reshaping of power.

Beyond its borders, Union forces maintained a naval blockade around the entire state and occupied major ports such as Cedar Key, Jacksonville, Key West, and Pensacola.

Florida mattered strategically to the Confederate war effort. Its cattle, saltworks, and ports fed the militias. Small skirmishes flared along the coasts and in the interior, including the Battle of Natural Bridge, the Battle of Marianna, and the Battle of Gainesville. The only large-scale, full conventional engagement in the state was the Battle of Olustee, fought near Lake City on February 20, 1864.

Olustee was Florida's bloodiest Civil War battle and the Confederacy's third-largest battle in 1864. Union forces, many of them newly raised U.S. Colored Troops, advanced inland from Jacksonville with the goal of disrupting Confederate supply lines and bringing Florida back under federal control. Confederate troops repelled the advance, inflicting heavy casualties and securing interior Florida for the remainder of the war.

1870-1900

Union occupation changed more than flags. Enslaved men, women, and children from surrounding plantations had already begun slipping toward federal lines as blue uniforms appeared along the coast. Emancipation made their presence permanent. Schools for freed children opened, and churches formed. The Freedmen's Bureau operated in the region, mediating labor contracts and disputes in a society being unevenly forced into a new order.

Reconstruction brought politics into the open. Black men registered to vote, and some held local office. It was a moment of fragile possibility. But the transformation was short-lived. By the mid-1870s, white Democratic "Redeemers" reasserted control across Florida. Federal commitment waned, and those perilous gains narrowed. What had opened in possibility began to close again. By the 1880s and 1890s, segregation hardened into law.

In St. Augustine, as across the South, Reconstruction was not a clean rebirth but a contested experiment. Freedom arrived. Equality did not.

The Seminoles who had remained in Florida continued in relative isolation through these decades. They traded hides and goods, maintained clan structures, and kept their distance from expanding railroads and towns. The United States largely ignored them—no longer a military threat, not yet a tourism curiosity. They existed outside the dominant narrative of postwar Florida, a remnant of resistance living in wetlands most Americans preferred not to enter.

Meanwhile, Florida itself was transforming. Railroads pushed south. Towns expanded, and tourism began reshaping coastal cities. Citrus groves multiplied. The peninsula that had once been dismissed as swamp and scrub was marketed as a winter paradise. Land speculation surged as developers described Florida as empty opportunity—rarely mentioning the layers of Native resistance, Black sanctuary, imperial contest, and forced removal beneath their survey lines.

By 1900, Florida was being reinvented as a modern American state—rebranded, repackaged, and largely stripped of its earlier identities. The Spanish century and a half, the sanctuary policies, Fort Mose, the Seminole resistance, and the Black frontier alliances—all receded from public memory. The dominant story compressed Florida into footnotes: a minor Civil War state, a late-joining member of the Union, and a vacationland.

But beneath the citrus groves and tract houses, the earlier history remained embedded in the landscape: coquina walls still scarred by cannon fire, river crossings once used by freedom seekers, and swamp trails that had confounded armies. The nineteenth century did not erase the past. It buried it under growth, development, and selective memory.

[1] Cusick, James G. (2003). The Other War of 1812: The Patriot War and the American Invasion of Spanish East Florida. Gainesville: University Press of Florida.
[2] Covington, James W. (1993). The Seminoles of Florida. Gainesville, Florida: University Press of Florida.
[3] Abram, Susan M. (2013) [2012]. "Native American Removal". In Dumenil, Lynn (ed.). The Oxford Encyclopedia of American Social History.
[4] Jon D. May (2009). "Horse, John (ca. 1812-1882)". OKState.org/. Oklahoma Historical Society: Encyclopedia of Oklahoma History & Culture.

Closing Thoughts

By the twentieth century, St. Augustine still stood—but it no longer stood at the center of anything. Railroads bypassed it for faster-growing ports, and political power shifted north and west. The city that had once anchored imperial defense and continental strategy became picturesque rather than pivotal. Coquina walls became tourist attractions. The oldest European-founded city in what is now the United States slowly became a curiosity.

Power does not just redraw borders. It rewrites beginnings.

As the United States industrialized and expanded, nineteenth-century historians began consolidating a usable national past. The story required clarity, moral simplicity, and English roots. Jamestown became the cradle of representative government, and Plymouth the birthplace of religious liberty. The Pilgrims fit Protestant America, and Virginia the Anglo political inheritance. These origins aligned neatly with language, race, and political continuity. A Spanish Catholic founding—multiracial, imperial, complex—did not.

St. Augustine complicated the narrative. It predated the Pilgrims by decades. It was shaped by Spaniards, Africans, both enslaved and free, and by Natives through both alliance and resistance. It did not flow cleanly into the

English colonial arc that culminated in 1776. And so it was minimized—not erased entirely, but localized. A regional story. A footnote on a tourist plaque. Not a foundational chapter. Colonial America's 14th and 15th colonies during the Revolutionary War are mostly ignored, if mentioned at all.

Identity is everything, and the United States now defined itself as an English-speaking republic born in rebellion against monarchy. Elevating a Spanish imperial outpost as America's first enduring city would have forced a broader admission: that the American story began not with thirteen colonies but with competing empires, Catholic missions, slave sanctuaries, Black militias, and Indigenous diplomacy. That beginning was harder to teach in a young nation seeking unity.

Textbooks followed power, and museums reflected funding. Public memory condensed around narratives that supported the dominant identity. Protestant over Catholic. English over Spanish. Anglo over multiracial frontier. Erasure, in this sense, was an act of construction. By simplifying the past, the nation stabilized itself and avoided confronting a more entangled beginning.

When you walk through Saint Augustine today, you move through a landscape that predates the national story most Americans were taught to recite. The coquina walls of the Castillo de San Marcos still hold the harbor. Parish registers in the Cathedral Basilica of St. Augustine still record baptisms, marriages, and burials in careful ink. The street grid—tight, defensive, intimate—was laid down generations before English brick took hold farther north.

But the city never vanished. Its walls and its records remain. Muster rolls, royal decrees, and mission registers still sit in archives in Florida and Spain. Beneath parking lots and courtyards, archaeology continues to surface ceramics, fortifications, and domestic traces that complicate the tidy origin myth. What changed was not the history, but the story Americans chose to tell about where they began.

And that choice shaped everything that followed.

Epilogue

If we begin the American story in St. Augustine rather than
Plymouth, the nation looks different from the outset. It was
not born in 1620 by religious dissenters seeking freedom. It
was born in 1565 in a collision of empires—Spanish
soldiers, Timucua communities, Africans, both enslaved
and free, missionaries, merchants, and rival European
powers circling the coastline. The first enduring European
city in what would become the United States is neither
English nor Protestant, nor culturally uniform. It is
imperial, Catholic, militarized, and multiracial from the
outset.

That shift unsettles the mythology of American
exceptionalism. It reminds us that the continent was not a
blank slate awaiting English settlement but was already
mapped into global rivalries and Indigenous networks.
Slavery did not arrive as an afterthought; Africans were
present in Florida decades before Jamestown. Religious
conflict was not peripheral; it shaped alliances,
conversions, and wars. If the American story starts here, it
begins as contested terrain—linguistically, culturally, and
politically.

Reframing the origin also reframes identity. Instead of
imagining the United States emerging cleanly from thirteen
colonies, we see a layered inheritance: Spanish
fortifications, Native resistance, Black militias, British
plantation systems, and American expansion. That

complexity does not weaken the story. It strengthens it by making it honest.

Origins matter because they determine who belongs. If the beginning is English and Protestant, then English Protestant institutions appear foundational and inevitable. If the beginning includes Spanish law, African sanctuary, Indigenous diplomacy, and imperial rivalry, then diversity is not a modern addition. It is structural. Multiculturalism is not a deviation from the founding; it is part of it.

There is responsibility in correction. Historical revision is often treated as political interference, but the greater distortion lies in omission. Restoring St. Augustine to the national narrative does not diminish Jamestown or Plymouth but widens the lens. A country confident in its identity can afford complexity. If we start here, the American experiment appears less like a sudden creation in 1776 and more like the product of centuries of negotiation, conflict, adaptation, and survival. That understanding does not undo the nation. It clarifies it.

Appendix

Florida timeline (starting with Spanish acquisition/claim)

1513 — Juan Ponce de León lands on Florida's Atlantic coast and claims the region for Spain ("La Florida").

1521 — Ponce de León attempts a settlement on Florida's southwest coast; it fails.

1526 — Spanish-led San Miguel de Gualdape (location debated, likely Georgia/Carolinas region) attempts colonization; collapses.

1539–1543 — Hernando de Soto expedition crosses Florida, reshaping Indigenous politics and accelerating disease impacts.

1559 — Tristán de Luna expedition establishes Pensacola Bay settlement attempt; ultimately abandoned.

1565 — St. Augustine founded by Pedro Menéndez de Avilés; becomes the oldest continuously occupied European-founded city in what is now the U.S.

1565 — Spain defeats the French at Fort Caroline (near today's Jacksonville), consolidating Spanish control in northeast Florida.

late 1500s–1600s — Spain builds the Florida mission system across North Florida and into Georgia; Indigenous alliances and conflicts reshape the region.

1672 — Construction begins on the Castillo de San Marcos in St. Augustine (completed 1695).

1702 — English forces from Carolina attack St. Augustine; the Castillo holds.

1738 — Fort Mose (Gracia Real de Santa Teresa de Mose) established near St. Augustine, a free Black settlement under Spain.

1763 — Spain cedes Florida to Great Britain (Treaty of Paris), in exchange for the return of Havana (captured by the British). Britain creates East Florida (capital: St. Augustine) and West Florida (capital: Pensacola).

1779–1781 — During the American Revolution, Spain (under Bernardo de Gálvez) captures British posts along the Gulf Coast; the campaign culminates in the Siege of Pensacola (1781).

1783 — Florida returns to Spain (Treaty of Paris). Spain again governs East and West Florida.

1810 — West Florida Rebellion; short-lived "Republic of West Florida."

1810–1813 — The U.S. gradually annexes parts of West Florida (between the Mississippi and Perdido Rivers).

1817–1818 — First Seminole War; Andrew Jackson invades Spanish Florida, pressuring Spain's control.

1819 — Adams–Onís Treaty signed: Spain agrees to cede Florida to the United States (effective later).

1821 — United States takes possession of Florida; becomes a U.S. territory.

1823 — Treaty of Moultrie Creek pushes Seminoles onto a central Florida reservation, intensifying conflict.

1835–1842 — Second Seminole War (one of the longest and costliest U.S.–Indigenous wars); large-scale forced removals, some Seminoles remain in Florida.

1845 — Florida becomes the 27th state (March 3).

1861–1865 — Civil War: Florida secedes and joins the Confederacy; key coastal sites shift hands; Union blockade hits trade.

1865–1877 — Reconstruction in Florida; major political and economic realignments.

1880s–1890s — Rail expansion (notably Henry Flagler on the east coast, Henry Plant on the west) drives tourism and development.

1900 — Hurricane strikes Galveston; (not Florida, but it catalyzes storm science and Gulf Coast attention; Florida's deadly storms soon follow).

1926 — Great Miami Hurricane devastates South Florida; ends much of the 1920s land boom.

1935 — Labor Day Hurricane (Florida Keys) kills hundreds, one of the strongest U.S. landfalls on record.

1940s–1960s — Rapid growth from air conditioning, highways, military bases; major migration into Florida.

1961 — First human spaceflight era begins; Florida becomes central via Cape Canaveral launches.

1964 — Civil Rights Act; Florida's schools and public accommodations continue contested desegregation.

1980 — Mariel boatlift brings a major influx of Cuban immigrants, reshaping Miami and state politics.

1992 — Hurricane Andrew devastates South Florida; transforms building codes and insurance markets.

2000 — Presidential election recount crisis centers on Florida's vote count.

2004–2005 — Multiple hurricanes (Charley, Frances, Ivan, Jeanne; then Katrina/Wilma impacts) hammer the state.

2016–2018 — Hurricanes Matthew, Irma, Michael cause major destruction; Michael devastates the Panhandle.

2020–2023 — Population growth accelerates; housing/insurance pressures intensify; Hurricane Ian (2022) is among the costliest U.S. disasters.

2024–present — Continued growth, climate/insurance stress, and infrastructure demands shape Florida's politics and economy.

Further Reading

Core books on St. Augustine and Spanish Florida

Eugene Lyon, The Enterprise of Florida: Pedro Menéndez de Avilés and the Spanish Conquest of 1565–1568 (University Press of Florida).

Paul E. Hoffman, A New Andalucia and a Way to the Orient: The American Southeast During the Sixteenth Century (LSU Press).

Amy Turner Bushnell, Situado and Sabana: Spain's Support System for the Presidio and Mission Provinces of Florida.

Michael V. Gannon, The Cross in the Sand: The Early Catholic Church in Florida, 1513–1870 (University Press of Florida).

Indigenous Florida and the mission world

Jerald T. Milanich, Florida Indians and the Invasion from Europe (University Press of Florida / Library Press at UF).

John H. Hann, A History of the Timucua Indians and Missions (University Press of Florida).

Africans in Spanish Florida and Fort Mose

Jane Landers, Black Society in Spanish Florida (University of Illinois Press).

Kathleen Deagan, Darcie MacMahon, and Jane Landers, Fort Mose: Colonial America's Black Fortress of Freedom (2nd ed.) (University Press of Florida).

Archaeology

Kathleen A. Deagan, Spanish St. Augustine: The Archaeology of a Colonial Creole Community.

Primary sources

National Park Service (Castillo de San Marcos) history and interpretive publications (good orientation + bibliographic trails).

St. Augustine Historical Society Research Library (translations of early church records back to 1594; colonial document copies).

Library of Congress, "East Florida Papers" collection (later Spanish period, with some earlier material included).

Study Guide

Part I — The World Before Spain

Key Ideas

- North America before European arrival was populated by complex societies.
- Chiefdoms and confederacies dominated the Southeast.
- Trade networks connected distant regions.

Important Groups

- Timucua
- Apalachee
- Guale
- Muscogee Confederacy

Key Questions

1. How were Southeastern societies organized politically?
2. What role did trade networks play before European arrival?
3. Why were chiefdoms vulnerable to sudden upheaval?

Discussion Topic

Compare Southeastern chiefdoms with the political organization of European states in the 1500s.

Part II — The Age of Exploration

Key Figures

- Juan Ponce de León
- Lucas Vázquez de Ayllón
- Álvar Núñez Cabeza de Vaca

Key Events

- Early Spanish reconnaissance along the Atlantic and Gulf coasts.
- Failed settlement attempts such as San Miguel de Gualdape.
- Shipwreck survival stories that reshaped Spanish understanding of North America.

Key Questions

1. Why was Spain interested in North America despite its wealth in the Caribbean and Mexico?
2. Why did early colonization attempts fail?
3. What did explorers learn from Indigenous societies?

Discussion Topic

How did early failures shape later Spanish strategies in Florida?

Part III — Conquest and Catastrophe

Key Expedition

Hernando de Soto

Key Themes

- Violent exploration and resource extraction.
- Cultural misunderstandings between Europeans and Indigenous societies.
- The spread of epidemic disease.

Key Locations

- Mississippi River
- Coosa Chiefdom

Key Questions

1. What was the goal of the De Soto expedition?
2. Why did Spanish expeditions often fail to establish stable colonies?
3. How did the expedition reshape the Southeast even though it produced no lasting settlement?

Discussion Topic

Was De Soto's expedition exploration, conquest, or disaster?

Part IV — Rivals and Religion

Major Rival Power

France

Key Event

French Huguenot settlement at Fort Caroline

Spanish Response

- Spain feared Protestant footholds in the New World.
- Military action and missionary expansion became intertwined.

Key Questions

1. Why did religion play such a major role in colonization?
2. How did European rivalries shape Florida's history?
3. Why did Spain see Protestant settlements as a direct threat?

Part V — The Founding of St. Augustine

Central Figure

Pedro Menéndez de Avilés

Key Event

Founding of St. Augustine

Key Developments

1. Establishment of a permanent Spanish colony.
2. Creation of a defensive network of forts and missions.
3. Development of alliances with Indigenous groups.

Key Questions

1. Why did St. Augustine succeed when earlier colonies failed?

2. What role did diplomacy with Indigenous communities play?

3. How did Spain maintain control in such a distant frontier?

Discussion Topic

Compare St. Augustine with Jamestown and Plymouth.

Part VI — A Multiracial Frontier

Important Community

Fort Mose

Fort Mose became the first legally recognized free Black settlement in what is now the United States.

Themes

- Spanish sanctuary policies for enslaved people fleeing English colonies.
- Intermarriage and cultural exchange.
- A frontier where Spanish, African, and Indigenous cultures blended.

Key Questions

1. Why did Spain offer sanctuary to enslaved people escaping English colonies?
2. How did Spanish Florida differ from English colonial societies?
3. What role did African soldiers play in defending the colony?

Major Themes of the Book

1. Forgotten Origins

The American story often begins with English colonies, but Spain established European America decades earlier.

2. Cultural Collision

Spanish, Indigenous, and African societies collided and blended in complex ways.

3. Empire on the Edge

Spanish Florida was a fragile frontier sustained through alliances and adaptation.

4. The Power of Historical Memory

The Spanish founding of America has often been minimized or overlooked in traditional narratives.

Suggested Essay Questions

1. Why has the Spanish founding of America been overshadowed in U.S. history?
2. How did Indigenous alliances shape the success of Spanish Florida?
3. What role did religion play in Spain's colonial strategy?
4. How did Spanish Florida become one of the earliest multicultural societies in North America?

Key Takeaway

Dawn of an Empire reframes the origins of American history. Long before English settlers arrived, Spain had already established cities, alliances, and communities that shaped the continent's earliest colonial era.

Acknowledgements

This book rests on the work of historians, archaeologists, and preservationists who have spent decades reconstructing Florida's layered past. Their scholarship and preservation of parish registers, military correspondence, excavation sites, and Spanish archives made it possible to tell this story with clarity rather than conjecture.

I am especially indebted to researchers who restored Fort Mose, the Spanish mission system, and the early Black and Seminole communities to the historical record. Their willingness to challenge inherited narratives reshaped how Florida's past is understood.

Gratitude is also due to the institutions that preserve this history: state archives, university collections, historical societies, and museum professionals who safeguard fragile documents and landscapes against time and development.

To readers who question simplified origin stories and look beyond the familiar thirteen-colony narrative—this work is for you. History is strongest when it is examined fully.

And finally, to those whose lives built St. Augustine— Native, African, European, free and enslaved—whose names are sometimes lost but whose presence endures in the walls, rivers, and soil of Florida. This book exists because they did.

Notes on Sources

This book is written for general readers, but it is built on the work of professional historians, archaeologists, and archivists.

Primary Sources

Spanish Florida generated an unusually rich paper trail. Much of what we know about St. Augustine, Fort Mose, and Florida's shifting empires comes from:

- Spanish colonial records: governors' letters, military dispatches, royal decrees, and administrative reports preserved in Spanish and Cuban archives and in published document collections.
- Parish registers and notarial records from St. Augustine: baptisms, marriages, burials, property transactions, wills, and court petitions that reveal the lives of free and enslaved people.
- British colonial records from the 1763–1784 period: land grants, correspondence, and Loyalist claims documenting East and West Florida as Britain's 14th and 15th mainland colonies.
- U.S. treaties and federal records: especially the Adams–Onís Treaty (1819) and removal-era treaties shaping Seminole history.

Archaeology and Material Evidence

Because many communities left limited written records—especially enslaved and marginalized groups—archaeology provides essential evidence. Excavations at Fort Mose and related colonial sites reveal housing patterns, foodways, trade goods, and daily life that do not always appear in official documents. The work of archaeologists and historical archaeologists is used throughout to anchor narrative claims in physical evidence.

Key Secondary Works

For Spanish Florida and Fort Mose, I relied heavily on major scholarly syntheses, including:

- Jane Landers' work on Black life in Spanish Florida and sanctuary policy
- Kathleen Deagan's decades of archaeological research on St. Augustine and Fort Mose
- Studies in The Florida Historical Quarterly and university-press monographs on British Florida, Loyalist migration, and the Second Spanish Period
- Scholarship on the Seminole Wars, maroon communities, and removal policy

What This Book Does Not Do

This is not an exhaustive academic history, and it does not attempt to cite every archival document in the narrative. Instead, it uses evidence to reconstruct the most consequential events and themes with accuracy and readability.

About the Author

Irene Loftin has spent more than 25 years as a writer working in storytelling and community outreach. Across that career, one principle has remained constant: stories shape what people remember—and what they overlook.

Before turning to long-form historical writing, she spent years working in community organizing and alongside grassroots organizations, helping local leaders amplify their voices and document the stories often overlooked in official narratives.

Her work has taken her far beyond archives and libraries. She has traveled throughout Africa, South America, and Asia—along with communities across the United States—meeting with residents in small towns and remote villages to listen, record, and share their stories. Whether in urban neighborhoods or rural settlements, her approach has remained the same: history begins with people, and the most meaningful stories are often local.

This global perspective informs her writing, which seeks to uncover the layered, human dimensions behind major historical events. She brings to her books a commitment to accuracy, narrative clarity, and a belief that the past is best understood when it includes the voices of those who lived it.

A Request from the Author

If this book spoke to you, a short book review is appreciated.

Reviews keep nonfiction history accessible to future generations and are greatly appreciated by authors and independent publishers like us.

The full catalog of books by Irene Loftin and Unbound Press can be found at: www.unboundpressbooks.com

More Books by <u>Unbound Press</u>

Frontier Chronicles: *Stories of the Contested American Frontier*

<u>Ghost Dance War</u>
The Last Uprising of Native Nations

<u>Women on the Prairie</u>
Stories of Grit, Survival and Unbroken Spirit

Spirits Unbroken: *Indigenous America Series*

<u>Echoes from the Eastern Shore</u>
Twelve Native American Chiefs and the Fight for the
Atlantic Homelands

Last Council Fires (coming soon)
Twelve Chiefs of the Colonial Southeast

Fault Lines: *Titanic Micro-histories*

<u>Steerage and Steel</u>
The True Story of Titanic's Crew and Immigrants

Ladies First
Titanic's Reckoning with Wealth and Worth

<u>American Silencer</u>
A History of Political Violence in America

America Uncovered

Women Between the Lines: *Overlooked Lives That Shaped History*

Mothers, Sisters, Soldiers, Spies
Women at War in American History

Troublesome Women
America's Whistleblowers, Cultural Pioneers, and the Women Who Changed the Rules

---

Hitler's Jewish Wife
The DNA of Eva Braun & The Secret of The Third Reich

Preview of Echoes from the Eastern Shore by Unbound Press Books

The following pages include a preview from Echoes from the Eastern Shore, available at bookstores and online at Amazon.com, Barnes and Noble, and www.unboundpressbooks.com

SPIRITS UNBROKEN

ECHOES FROM THE EASTERN SHORE

Twelve Native American Chiefs
and the Fight for the Atlantic Homelands

WARD MCLENDON

Introduction

The Atlantic coast was not a frontier waiting to be discovered. It was a homeland—densely inhabited, politically complex, and governed by nations with long-established systems of law, diplomacy, trade, and war. When Europeans arrived along its shores, they entered an existing world, not an empty one.

This volume examines that world through the lives of twelve Native American chiefs whose leadership shaped the earliest centuries of sustained contact along the Atlantic seaboard. Their stories span the Gulf of Maine, Southern New England, the Hudson River corridor, the Mid-Atlantic river systems, and the Chesapeake Tidewater. Together, they reveal how Indigenous nations confronted an invasion that unfolded unevenly yet relentlessly, pressing inland from the sea.

The period covered here is often framed in American history as a story of settlement and founding. From the Indigenous perspective, it was a period of escalating pressure—marked by epidemics that preceded colonization itself, followed by trade dependencies, territorial encroachment, warfare, forced treaties, and displacement.

These forces did not arrive all at once, nor did they affect every nation in the same way. Geography mattered, as did timing, alliances, internal divisions, and the strategies adopted by individual leaders.

Leadership in Indigenous societies was neither uniform nor absolute. Authority was shaped by kinship, council consensus, spiritual responsibility, and the ability to persuade rather than command. Chiefs had obligations to their people, not sovereign power over them. Decisions to fight, negotiate, relocate, or accommodate were constrained by factors beyond any one leader's control. Understanding those constraints is essential to understanding the choices recorded in colonial sources—and the silences where those sources fail.

Readers will encounter familiar events—alliances with European powers, cycles of trade and dependency, and wars labeled as "Indian" conflicts in colonial records. These labels obscure the fact that Indigenous nations rarely responded to a single empire alone. French, English, Dutch, and later American interests collided along the coast, and Native leaders navigated those rivalries with strategic intent. Some sought balance through diplomacy. Others chose resistance when accommodation failed. None operated in isolation.

The Atlantic homelands were also linked to powerful inland networks. The Haudenosaunee Confederacy, river-based nations such as the Lenape and Susquehannock, and interior peoples of Virginia shaped coastal outcomes even when they lived far from the sea. Trade routes, military alliances, and population movements tied the coast to the interior, and this volume treats these connections as central rather than peripheral.

Colonial records dominate the written archive for this period and pose inherent challenges. Many accounts were produced by missionaries, traders, or officials whose priorities distorted their observations. Indigenous voices often appear only indirectly, filtered through translation or recorded only when they intersected with colonial interests. Where possible, this volume draws on Indigenous oral histories, later tribal scholarship, and archaeological evidence to correct or complicate those records.

This book does not present its subjects as tragic inevitabilities or symbolic figures standing in for an entire people. They were political actors making decisions in real time, with incomplete information and limited options.

Some choices resulted in short-term survival at long-term cost. Others led to catastrophic loss. Judging those outcomes without understanding the conditions under which they were made risks repeating the moral simplifications of earlier histories.

The chapters that follow do not tell a single story of Native America. They tell many stories—of confederacies forged and fractured, of land defended and lost, of diplomacy attempted and betrayed, and of cultures adapting under pressure. What unites them is not defeat but endurance.

Despite centuries of displacement and erasure, the nations discussed in this volume did not disappear. They persist.

Echoes from the Eastern Shores opens the Spirits Unbroken series because the Atlantic homelands were the first place where these pressures converged and the longest where they were sustained. The leaders profiled here confronted the initial shock of invasion and its generational aftermath. Their stories form the foundation for understanding what followed as colonization moved inland and westward.

This is neither the beginning nor the conclusion of Native history. It is the record of a turning point—when Indigenous nations along the Atlantic coast were forced to defend their homelands against forces that would reshape an entire continent, and when survival itself became an act of leadership.

Chapter 1 — A Coast in Motion

•◦ ◦•

*"We don't inherit the earth from our ancestors, we borrow it from
our children."*

—Native American Proverb

The Atlantic Homelands

ON A LATE AUTUMN morning in 1620, Massasoit stood near the edge of the water and watched the sea.

The shoreline was quiet. The tide was moving out across the flats, leaving dark bands of kelp and wet sand that reflected the pale sky. The air carried the smell of salt and decaying leaves, the season already turning. For weeks, perhaps longer, his people had spoken of a ship anchored beyond the reach of the surf—a large, square-rigged vessel riding deeper in the water than the fishing boats that sometimes appeared along the coast.

This ship was different.

The Wampanoag were no strangers to Europeans. Long before this moment, they had traded with passing crews, watched ships come and go, and heard stories of failed settlements—outposts abandoned after hunger, sickness, or conflict made them untenable. Foreign visitors were not new. What was new was permanence.

The vessel offshore did not leave.

From a distance, Massasoit could see the signs: the careful anchoring, the small boats moving back and forth, and the deliberate pace of men who expected to stay. This was not a trading expedition or a fishing crew waiting for the weather to turn. This was a settlement in motion.

Illustration, English ship

The timing could not have been worse.

Only a few years earlier, sickness had swept through the coastal villages with devastating force. Entire communities had been emptied. Fields went untended. Councils lost elders whose authority had anchored political life for generations. The Wampanoag Confederacy—once strong, expansive, and secure—had been weakened at precisely the moment when its rivals were not. To the west and south, the Narragansett remained powerful. To the east and north, other nations watched closely as they recalculated the balance of power.

Massasoit understood what the ship represented. New people meant new pressures. They could become allies—or enemies.

He also understood that the moment demanded restraint. Strength alone would not determine what followed. Survival would depend on judgment.

For thousands of years before that ship appeared on the horizon, the peoples of this coast had lived in a world shaped by water, seasons, and negotiated boundaries. The land the English would soon call New England was not an untouched wilderness. It was a managed landscape, shaped by agriculture, controlled burns, fishing weirs, trade routes, and diplomacy.

It was not unoccupied.

They called it Wabanaki—Dawnland—the place where the sun rises first, where rivers run cold and fast from the interior and spread into bays thick with fish and fog. The people later gathered under the label Wabanaki Confederacy were not a single tribe but an alliance of neighboring nations—bound by marriage ties, trade routes, shared enemies, and the hard arithmetic of survival once Europeans arrived in force. In that world, identity was anchored to watersheds and seasons: the river you traveled, the coast you harvested, the portage you carried across when the ice broke, and the canoes you went back in.

The Wolastoqiyik, often called the Maliseet in older English sources, were the people of the Wolastoq, the "bright" or "shining" river Europeans renamed the Saint John. Their homeland was a long river corridor running through today's New Brunswick into northern Maine, a place where power came from controlling movement: who could pass upriver, who could trade, who could be fed in winter, who could be warned in time.

To know the Wolastoqiyik is to picture birchbark canoes gliding along tributaries, villages tied to the rhythms of salmon and moose, and a politics shaped by proximity — Mi'kmaq to the east, Penobscot to the west, Passamaquoddy to the south — neighbors who could be allies one season and rivals the next, depending on what the French and English offered and demanded.

South of them, where the coastline breaks into coves and islands, and the water turns brackish, lived the Passamaquoddy — Peskotomuhkatiyik — a people whose center of gravity was the bay that still carries their name.

Their homeland straddled what would become the U.S.–Canada border, but their lives didn't: the sea and the shore were the real map. Passamaquoddy communities were sustained by marine abundance and by the certainty that fishing places—villages like Sipayik (Pleasant Point)—were not merely "locations" but living archives, where families returned year after year to work, feast, argue, decide, and remember. In early contact history, that coastal position mattered. It put them in the path of fishing fleets and traders early on and made them essential brokers in the shifting diplomacy of the Northeast.

The Abenaki—Wôbanaki in their own language—formed another crucial span of the Dawnland, stretching across river valleys and interior routes that linked the Gulf of Maine to the St. Lawrence. Here, the usual shorthand—Eastern Abenaki and Western Abenaki—is less about two separate "tribes" than about language and geography: Eastern Abenaki communities were concentrated more in what is now Maine, while Western Abenaki communities were centered more in Quebec, Vermont, and New Hampshire, tied into the north–south corridors of the Champlain and Connecticut systems.

In Wabanaki politics, the Abenaki mattered because they occupied the region's connective tissue—routes armies used, routes refugees fled along, and routes trade followed—so they were often the ones forced to decide, again and again, whether a new alliance offered protection or only postponed the next blow

The Wampanoag Confederacy governed a broad territory of coastal plains, rivers, and woodlands. Villages shifted with the seasons. Cornfields were planted and harvested with precision. Fishing runs were anticipated and regulated. Authority rested not in a single ruler but in networks of sachems and councils, bound by kinship, obligation, and custom. Diplomacy was essential, especially as European rivalries between France and England began to disrupt existing Indigenous power balances.

This was not a static society. It adapted constantly to climate, internal rivalry, and external pressure. Trade connected coastal peoples with those living inland. News traveled faster than outsiders could grasp. Decisions were weighed collectively, with memory stretching back generations. These were not scattered villages operating in isolation. They were nations—some small, some expansive—refined over generations.

Across North America, Indigenous nations had built similarly complex worlds. From the Gulf of Maine to the Chesapeake, from the Great Lakes to the plains beyond, societies rose and fell, confederacies formed and fractured, and systems of governance evolved long before Europeans began keeping records. Many Indigenous societies were organized around rivers and shorelines that functioned as transportation corridors, food sources, and defensive boundaries. Hunting territories and sacred spaces were regulated through custom and negotiation.

Leadership was situational and relational, not absolute. Authority flowed from consensus, lineage, spiritual responsibility, and the ability to persuade rather than command. These were not accidental cultures but the result of millennia of lived experience.

The arrival of Europeans did not introduce history to the continent. It introduced disruption.

Disease arrived first, moving faster than settlers, killing without negotiation or warning. Then came trade, which brought tools and weapons alongside dependency. Then came settlements—fenced, fortified, permanent. What had once been occasional contact hardened into occupation.

Massasoit had no way of knowing how far this process would go. No one did. What he could see, standing on the shore, was that the old balance had already begun to shift. The presence offshore posed a question to his people and to the region itself: resist, accommodate, or attempt something in between?

That decision would shape who lived, who ruled, and who remained.

In the years that followed, Massasoit would choose accommodation—not out of trust or naïveté, but calculation. He would attempt to fold the newcomers into an existing political world, to make them one power among many rather than a force apart. For a time, it would work.

But the ship on the horizon marked the beginning of a new phase in the history of the Atlantic homelands—one in which the choices available to Indigenous leaders narrowed with each passing decade, and in which survival itself became a form of resistance.

This book begins there, at the edge of the water, before outcomes were certain and before American history had a name. It is the story of the leaders who faced that horizon first, and of the nations who fought—by diplomacy, by war, and by endurance—to remain on the land they had always called home.

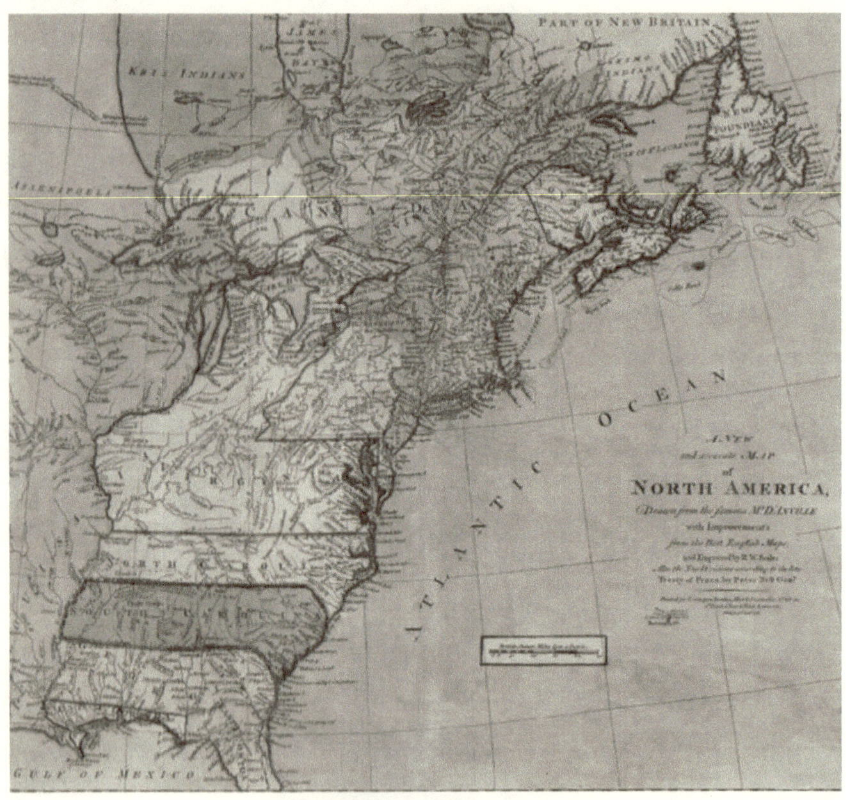

Illustration of Atlantic Coast

Their world did not disappear with contact. It collided with
it.

The Many Nations

The Hudson Valley and Long Island formed another
political crossroads. Here, numerous closely related
communities governed distinct territories while navigating
the influence of larger inland powers—most notably the
Haudenosaunee Confederacy. The Five (later Six) Nations
wielded enormous influence over trade, warfare, and
diplomacy across the Northeast, shaping outcomes along
the coast even though their villages lay far inland.

South of New England, the Lenape homelands along the
Delaware River basin sustained a sophisticated river-based
society that linked the Atlantic coast to the interior. Lenape
communities regulated access to land and waterways
through negotiation and custom rather than written deeds.
This distinction would later prove disastrous.

In the Chesapeake region, the Powhatan Confederacy was
among the most politically centralized Indigenous systems
encountered by Europeans. Dozens of communities were
bound together by tribute, alliance, and force, forming a
regional power that initially dictated the terms of English
survival in Virginia. Along the Eastern Shore and upriver,
other nations navigated the expanding gravitational pull of
English settlement.

This diversity matters. There was no single "Native response" to colonization because there was no single Native world to begin with.

Contact Was Not a Moment

The term "contact" suggests a single encounter: ships arriving, hands shaking, worlds meeting. In reality, contact was a process that unfolded unevenly over decades—and often began before sustained settlement took root.

Early Atlantic Contacts

Seasonal European fishing fleets began working the rich cod grounds off Newfoundland and the Grand Banks in the late 1400s, with English, French, Spanish, and Portuguese crews crossing the Atlantic every summer.[1] In the late 1400s and early 1500s, Iberian and later English and French expeditions began crossing the Atlantic, initially seeking routes to Asia and valuable resources.

These fishermen came ashore to dry fish, cut timber, and take on water. In some places, this meant trading in fish, furs, and tools; in others, Indigenous peoples such as the Beothuk tried to avoid face-to-face meetings and instead scavenged abandoned European fishing stations.[2]

By the late 1500s, hundreds of boats sailed into these waters each year. European presence shifted from short, sporadic visits to more organized ventures centered on trade. Fur traders in the north established posts and relied on Indigenous partners who supplied pelts, food, geographic knowledge, and military support, while receiving metal tools, cloth, and other goods that were integrated into Native economies and diplomacy.

Missionaries, especially Spanish in the south and French in the north, established missions that were often the first permanent European institutions in some regions, introducing new religious pressures and attempting to gather Indigenous people into mission towns. These missions, posts, and small forts became places where languages, beliefs, and technologies mixed, and where alliances and rivalries between Indigenous nations and European powers first sparked conflict and compromise.

Colonies and Contagions

Permanent colonies quickly followed: Jamestown in 1607, Quebec in 1608, and Plymouth in 1620, with further English settlements in New England and along the mid-Atlantic coast through the 1600s. New Netherland was founded by the Dutch in 1624, with New Amsterdam established in 1625; the English colony of Maryland was established in 1632–1634, each tightening European claims on Indigenous homelands.

These colonies arrived not as neutral neighbors but as expansionist systems fueled by land hunger. They claimed land, demanded labor or tribute, and drew Indigenous nations into European wars and imperial rivalries, even as

Native communities tried to keep their distance. European concepts of property, sovereignty, and inheritance were fundamentally incompatible with Indigenous land use and governance. Oral and conditional agreements were later recorded as permanent transfers. Alliances forged for survival were treated as submissions.

Trade further complicated the landscape. Metal tools, firearms, and cloth reshaped daily life and warfare, creating dependencies that European powers exploited. Control of trade networks became as critical as control of territory. Indigenous leaders were forced to balance immediate material needs with long-term autonomy, often without knowing which choice would be fatal.

Pathogens traveled along the same networks: Native traders who met Europeans on the seacoast or in early mission settlements could carry measles, influenza, and smallpox to distant villages days or weeks away, long before anyone in those communities ever saw a European face.

Smallpox became one of the most destabilizing forces in the Atlantic homelands, as epidemic disease preceded large-scale settlement, weakening communities before they fully understood the source of the catastrophe. The demographic losses reshaped politics: succession crises emerged, towns consolidated or relocated, alliances shifted, and the balance of power among neighboring nations changed.

These epidemics also intensified colonial pressure. As populations fell and communities were forced to reorganize, Europeans increasingly treated disrupted land use as abandonment. They used disease-driven instability to push for land cessions, "protections," or permanent settlement.

The first major smallpox pandemic in the Americas swept out from the Caribbean around 1518–1525, killing enormous numbers of Indigenous people on the islands and then in Mesoamerica, where one epidemic in 1520–1521 may have killed a third to half of the population. Through the 1500s and early 1600s, waves of smallpox, measles, influenza, and other infections continued to strike Native communities across the hemisphere, often in rapid succession, leaving no time for recovery between outbreaks.

In eastern North America, for example, a devastating epidemic—sometimes called "the Great Dying"—swept through Indigenous villages in southern New England between 1616 and 1619, likely killing the majority of people in some coastal areas several years before the Mayflower arrived in 1620.[3]

By the mid-1600s, repeated epidemics had already reshaped the human landscape in many regions, leaving behind what later colonists wrongly imagined to be "empty" or "widowed" lands.

These losses did more than reduce numbers; they undermined governance and social stability across many Indigenous nations. Deaths among elders, healers, warriors, and diplomatic leaders disrupted the transmission of knowledge, weakened existing alliances, and opened the door to internal tensions and external pressures.

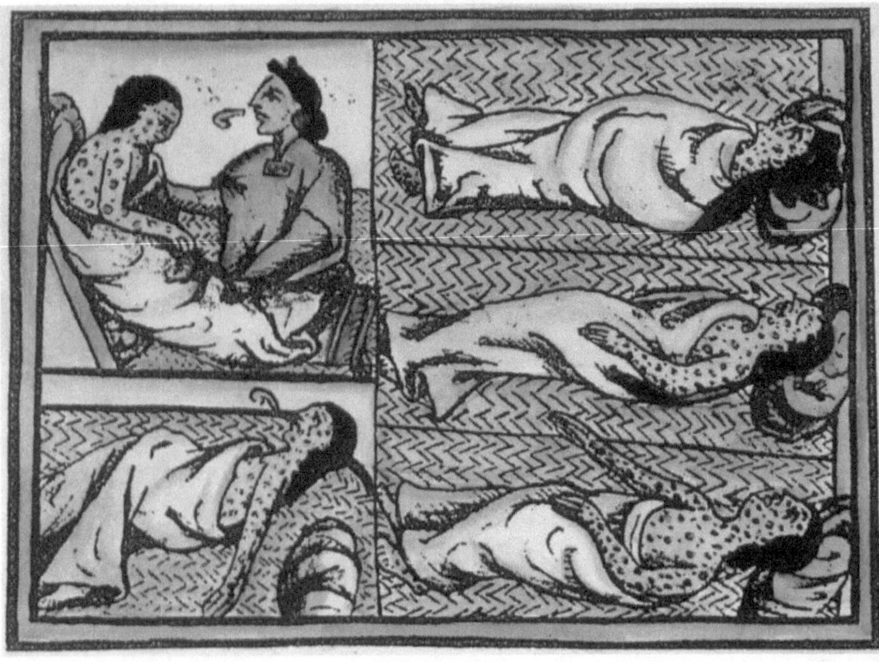

Smallpoxl Original illustration by unknown 16th-century artist, Public Domain.

With fewer people to hunt, farm, or trade, and with neighboring groups suffering unevenly, competition for remaining hunting grounds, trade routes, and safe territories often intensified. Treaties were negotiated by communities still reeling from population loss. Wars were fought by nations already weakened by illness. Alliances were forged in a landscape where survival itself had become uncertain.

By the time sustained colonization accelerated along the Atlantic coast, Indigenous societies had already endured a demographic and political shock that fundamentally altered the terms of contact.

Leadership Under Pressure

Indigenous leadership was tested not only by external threats but also by internal strain. Population loss had weakened traditional authority, and younger leaders challenged elders. Factions emerged over whether to resist, negotiate, relocate, or align with one colonial power against another. These divisions were not signs of weakness; they were symptoms of societies under unprecedented stress.

Colonial records often portray Native leaders as inconsistent or unreliable for failing to deliver permanent outcomes. This misrepresents Indigenous political reality. Chiefs were accountable to councils and communities, not empowered to bind their people indefinitely. A treaty made under duress did not erase future resistance. Accommodation did not signal surrender.

Leaders were forced to operate within these constraints. They were not free agents. They were mediators between worlds, responsible for immediate survival and long-term

continuity in circumstances that allowed for neither
certainty nor safety.

A Shared Turning Point

What united the Atlantic Homelands was not culture,
language, or political structure but timing. These nations
faced the earliest and most sustained pressures of
European colonization. The decisions made along the
coast—alliances formed, wars fought, treaties signed,
migrations forced—shaped the trajectory of colonization
across the continent.

As European expansion reached inland in force, the
Atlantic world had already been transformed. The
strategies that succeeded or failed there became precedents
elsewhere. The cost of miscalculation was already evident.

Across the continent, Indigenous peoples blended older
traditions with new realities—reshaping economies,
diplomacy, and spiritual life—so that, even after centuries
of upheaval, their communities, languages, and political
goals endure today. This broader story of contact is one of
profound loss but also of ongoing negotiation, survival,
and creativity in the face of rapidly changing forces.

Their stories, and the stories of the leaders who follow, are
rooted in the world outlined here—a world that did not
vanish with contact, but was irrevocably altered by it.

[1] Cornelius J. Jaenen, Friend and Foe: Aspects of French–Amerindian Cultural Contact in the Sixteenth and Seventeenth Centuries (Toronto: McClelland and Stewart, 1976), 98–99.
[2] Colin G. Calloway, First Peoples: A Documentary Survey of American Indian History (Baltimore: Johns Hopkins University Press, 1997).
[3] Heather Whipps, "How Smallpox Changed the World," LiveScience, June 23, 2008.